EVERT W. BETH

ASPECTS OF
MODERN LOGIC

D. REIDEL PUBLISHING COMPANY / DORDRECHT-HOLLAND

MODERNE LOGICA

Published by Van Gorkum & Comp. N.V., Assen, 1967
with support of the Prins Bernhard Fonds
Translated from the Dutch by Dr. D. H. J. de Jongh and Susan de Jongh-Kearl

Library of Congress Catalog Card Number 79–135102

SBN 90 277 0173 3

A NOTE ON THE EDITING

This book stems from an unfinished manuscript which was found after the death of Professor Beth. The manuscript was accompanied by a detailed description of the subjects, which the author had wanted to discuss in this book, and the order as he had planned it.

The first four chapters were almost ready for publication. Together they form a coherent exposition of the method of semantic and deductive tableaux designed by Professor Beth. To these four chapters we added the chapter which had been projected as the eighth, 'About the so-called thought machine'. The first part of the book, consisting of these five chapters, has thus become a coherent presentation on logic in the narrower sense.

The remaining chapters had not been worked out, but the texts of three articles, the contents of which combine well with some of the unfinished chapters, and which the author very probably meant to utilize in preparing these chapters, had been joined to the manuscript by Professor Beth. These articles appear here as the Chapters VI, VII and VIII. We added to this also the two articles which appear here as Chapters IX and X. These five unchanged articles form the second part of the book. This explains why some chapters in part 2 have not been subdivided into sections, while part 1 is consistently so subdivided.

We have seen fit to make some annotations to elucidate the text. These are denoted by one or more asterisks.

E. M. BARTH

J. J. A. MOOIJ

ACKNOWLEDGEMENTS

In a conversation which I had with Drs. E. M. Barth in 1965, she brought to my attention the desirability of publishing posthumously a manuscript entitled *Aspects of Modern Logic*, by my deceased husband, although it was in an unfinished state. Together with Dr. J. J. A. Mooij, at my request, she prepared this book for publication. To both I express here my gratitude for the care and devotion with which they conducted this task, which, among other things, consisted of making the manuscript ready for press.

I am very thankful to Drs. H. C. Doets for the assistance he gave in compiling the bibliography, the author and subject indexes, and for reading the printed proofs.

For the second time I have the pleasure of expressing my indebtedness to the Prins Bernhard Fonds, which, after its financial contribution for the publication of *Science, A Road to Wisdom*, has now similarly subsidized *Aspects of Modern Logic*.

Also I thank the Koninklijke Nederlandse Akademie van Wetenschappen of Amsterdam, the Uitgeversmaatschappij P. Noordhoff N.V. of Groningen, the Uitgeverij Het Spectrum N.V. of Utrecht/Antwerp, the editors of *Euclides* and the editors of the *Algemeen Nederlands Tijdschrift voor Wijsbegeerte en Psychologie* for their permission to reproduce previously published studies in this book; for more detailed information I refer to 'Sources'.

Finally I wish to thank Dr. D. H. J. de Jongh for his spontaneity in accepting the task of translating this book into English. Also I want to express my gratitude to Mrs. S. de Jongh-Kearl for the advice she gave her husband during the translation.

C. P. C. BETH-PASTOOR

CONTENTS

PART II

PART I

PART I

INTRODUCTION

It is common to consider an area of science as a system of real or supposed truths which not only continuously extends itself, but also needs periodical revision and therefore tests the inventive capacity of each generation of scholars anew. It sounds highly implausible that a science at one time would be completed, that at that point within its scope there would be no problems left to solve. Indeed, the solution of a scientific problem inevitably raises new questions, so that our eagerness for knowledge will never find lasting satisfaction.

Nevertheless there is one science which seems to form an exception to this rule, formal logic, the theory of rigorous argumentation. It seems to have reached the ideal endpoint of every scientific aspiration already very shortly after its inception; using the work of some predecessors, Aristotle, or so it is at least assumed by many, has brought this branch of science once and for all to a conclusion.

Of course this doesn't sound that implausible. We apparently know what rigorous argumentation is; otherwise various sciences, in particular pure mathematics, would be completely impossible. And if we know what rigorous argumentation is, then it cannot be difficult to trace once and for all the rules which govern it. The unique subject of formal logic would therefore entail that this science, in variance with the rule which holds for all other sciences, has been able to reach completion at a certain point in history.

This was the way, at least, in which during the last two centuries most philosophers reasoned. They also observed that attempts at revision or supplementation of Aristotle's work had yielded only little results. This, too, affirmed the opinion that the doctrine of rigorous argumentation had been brought to a conclusion by Aristotle, so that further investigations in this area might be called superfluous and useless. Immanuel Kant (1724–1804) has expressed the opinion sketched here very clearly: in the second printing of his *Kritik der reinen Vernunft,* he calls it remarkable that logic since Aristotle's time hasn't been able to make one step forward and therefore is seemingly completed and concluded. Even in our days one often encounters this opinion.

One will hardly be able to produce a more glaring example of the tenacity with which an error can maintain itself, when it only sounds sufficiently plausible and is moreover supported by the prestige of a great name. The opinion rendered above is not only completely incorrect, it was already obsolete when Kant formulated it. Formal logic has gone through a continuous development which begins already with the forma-tion of the so-called peripatetic school by Aristotle's followers, and which, for the time being, is closed off by the decay of medieval scholastics. As great figures in this period one can name Theophrastus, the successor of Aristotle as leader of the school founded by him, Chrysippus, the stoic, Boëthius, better known by his *Consolatio philosophiae*, Petrus Abaelardus, the adventurous scholastic, Petrus Hispanus, who became Pope John XXI, and William Ockham. Through their work formal logic was not only strongly extended, but also significantly deepened.

All this, however, passed into oblivion with the birth of a new mentality in the scientific world which replaced abstract reasoning by experiments and by the quantitative analysis of the observed phenomena. For logic one was therefore dependent on Aristotle again, whose authority in the circles of the Roman Catholic theologians appeared unassailable and whose prestige was soon felt also in Protestant theology.

And now it is remarkable how soon formal logic found new roads. A new development started which continues into the present. With Descartes one finds only a few indications of that; with Geulincx, the Flemish philosopher who was Professor at Leiden and by whom two highly curious writings about logic are known, the medieval tradition still probably has an after-effect.

The history of modern logic is usually taken to begin with G. W. Leibniz (1646–1716), who by the way owes his fame more to his ideas about metaphysics and epistemology than to his investigations in the area of formal logic. For modern logic Leibnitz is mainly important because of the program he drew up for its development. It is true that the contributions he and his immediate followers could make to the realiza-tion of this program were fragmentary. But this could hardly be other-wise; here a task had been put to which generations would have to work.

This Kant and Hegel, and with them many others, alas, did not appreciate, and when Leibnitz and his supporters did not immediately appear equal to this task, they drew from that the rash conclusion that Leibnitz's program was not capable of realization, and that formal logic had, at least in principle, been brought to a conclusion through Aristotle and his first followers.

Meanwhile, nevertheless, the development of logic, albeit quietly, continued. In the middle of the eighteenth century Ploucquet and Lambert in Germany, and towards the middle of the nineteenth century De Morgan and Boole in England, continued the work taken up by Leibnitz; already Boole establishes a relationship with the abstract direction in mathematics emerging in his time. Towards the end of the nineteenth century the movement begins to show a more international character. In the U.S. Peirce and his students are working, in Italy Peano with a staff of collaborators, in England Venn, and in Germany Frege and Schröder. Frege and Peano establish the relationship with mathematical foundational studies which turned out to be necessary when the abstract direction became more obvious. Of all these investigators Frege must be called the greatest, but the significance of his work was recognized and understood only later.

The First International Congress for Philosophy, held in 1900 in Paris, suddenly put the new development in the field of formal logic in the spotlight. This led, especially in France, to fierce debates to which are bound the names of Couturat, Henri Poincaré and Bertrand Russell.

Since then the practice of modern logic, now often designated as *mathematical*, or better, *symbolic logic* (the term *logistics* has not been able to maintain itself), has steadily increased. At the same time, however, as a consequence of the otherwise very stimulating ties with mathematical foundational studies, and with modern abstract mathematics, a specialism has developed which starts to impede the very desirable distribution of the often very surprising insights which in the course of the years the investigations have yielded.

From this, and from the continuing existence of the earlier sketched views of Kant and many others, it can be explained that many who have something to do with formal logical problems still manage with the so-called traditional formal logic founded on the authority of Aristotle, which, although completely obsolete, is still treated in many textbooks.

The historical facts discussed are, however, in direct contradiction with the opinion expressed by Kant. Twice in the course of history it has turned out that the formal logic of Aristotle is not a completed science, but that it bears the germs of further development; it would of course be foolish to assess the accomplishments of Aristotle as a logician less highly on the basis of that.

Even though it is not really necessary, it can be demonstrated by the following example, originating with Aristotle's contemporary Eubulides of Milete, and handed down to us by Cicero, that Aristotle had not brought all formal logical problems to solution. Someone asserts: "*I am lying*". Is this proposition true or is it false? If the proposition is true, then the speaker is indeed lying, and therefore what he says has to be false. But if the proposition is false, then the speaker is not lying, and therefore he speaks the truth; the assertion he makes is therefore true.

It is difficult to make a sound objection to this reasoning, and yet the conclusion is contrary to one of the basic principles of Aristotle's formal logic. This, namely, proceeded from the assumption that each proposition asserted (contrary to a proposition, the content of which is a question, an order, a promise or a judgement), is either true or false, but can never be simultaneously false and true. Traditional logic has never succeeded in solving this puzzle convincingly; modern logic has succeeded in that only around 1930.

In the practice of formal logic there have always been three guiding motives: interest for the problems of logic as such, the clarification of the inner relationship of certain deductive disciplines (usually mathematical theories), and the need for a directive for critical thinking (notably about philosophical and political systems). In the last decades formal logic has also turned out to be important for the theory of digital computers; otherwise the emphasis, however, falls on the first two motives, which is, alas, detrimental to the application of formal logic as a directive for critical thinking. This is related to the bonds of modern formal logic, abstract mathematics and mathematical foundational studies, and to the specialistic character which symbolic logic has consequently more and more obtained.

Now, by this development, formal logic has not in the least lost its suitability as a directive for critical thinking; the contrary is true. In the way of exposition common at present, however, the subjects which would deserve attention with respect to this objective come to lie far apart. Therefore one cannot get to know these subjects without immersing oneself in all kinds of problems which are exclusively important for those who study logic for its own sake, or for the sake of mathematical foundational studies. There are some introductory handbooks which don't deal with this kind of specialistic problems, but these remain too superficial to offer a trustworthy directive for critical thinking.

In this connection also a protest has to be entered against the often-defended opinion that one would acquire logical insight just by scientific study. It is true that in a scientific argument one conforms more than elsewhere to the demands of logic, and one will doubtlessly be able to acquire this excellent habit by scientific study, but even in mathematics an *express* appeal to logic occurs only extremely rarely. One usually comes to such an appeal only when it is already too late; that is to say, when one is compelled to accept a conclusion, the falsity of which is flagrantly obvious. It is clear that such an incidental appeal to logic will in itself be able to contribute very little to the acquisition of logical insight. Also in the field of logic, a more than superficial insight can be obtained only through a systematic study. Such a systematic study, though, turns out to entail quite a number of difficulties.

The basis of that, it occurs to me, is to be found in the fact that generally the right *method of instruction* is lacking. To procure the required insight it is by no means sufficient ot gather those subjects which are important for formal logic as a directive for critical thinking. The reader should at the same time acquire such a proficiency that the can really apply the resources put at this disposal by logic, but above all he has to learn to put so much faith as well in the reliability of these resources as in his own proficiency, that he will add with conviction the conclusions he derives to his mental assets. For that, especially, a certain measure of insight in the foundations on which formal logic rests is needed.

At the same time it has to be observed that although it may be true that modern formal logic yields a trustworthy directive for critical thinking, it is not in the least able to *compel* somebody to think critically; so the readiness to think critically has to be presupposed of the reader.

In the following chapters I have made an attempt to realize the program sketched above. For that purpose I have been led mainly by three considerations. In the first place the availability of a trustworthy directive for critical thinking will be able to strengthen the mental fiber and notably the resistance against contemporary irrationalism. Secondly, during the last years the construction of symbolic logic has been simplified to such an extent that the chances for success have been increased considerably. Thirdly, an attempt to promote critical thinking results naturally from my previous philosophical work.

The framework of my argument naturally had to correspond to the general objective just described. A synthetic exposition of the material, which would have consisted of the development of a closed system of formal logic, would hardly have been proper here. It wouldn't do either, however, to put before the reader a sort of recipe book.

I therefore sought a middle course and have finally decided on a more analytical treatment, which proceeds in some rotations. First the fundamental problems of formal logic are brought closer to the reader. Next the most important parts of formal logic are treated more systematically and in more detail. After that come supplementary considerations as well as examples of logical analysis. I have only aspired to completeness in relation to whatever was needed with regard to the restricted objective.

I would have rather refrained from the usual appeal to infantile illustrations. Alas, I have not succeeded in avoiding it everywhere; but I have restricted myself to the utmost on this point. On the other hand I have, of course, had to impose some moderation on myself as to the level of rigor. I have marked some passages with a § to indicate that the reader can, if so desired, skip them without interrupting the continuity.

E. W. BETH

Amsterdam/Maarn, February 17 – June 20, 1962

CHAPTER I

THE FUNDAMENTAL CRITERION FOR
THE SOUNDNESS OF ARGUMENTS

1. INTRODUCTION

This book is meant for readers who are prepared to think critically, and the author is therefore prepared for his exposition to be read critically. On the other hand it is rather meaningless to take up a book like this if one is not prepared to give the writer a certain measure of trust. This need makes itself felt especially, when certain questions arise in the reader which the author seems to overlook.

Indeed, it is impossible for the author to foresee all questions which at a certain moment can arise in a reader. And in the extent to which he foresees these questions, he can still deal with them only one by one. Into which questions he will go, and in which order, and in which manner, he will have to decide on the basis of his knowledge and experience. For the rest one will have to leave him the freedom to pass some questions by without comment, or delay their discussion until later. Sometimes he will prefer to state the answer to a problem dogmatically, or even to urge the reader not to ask certain questions at all.

I immediately make use of the authority claimed here to advise the reader urgently, in the judgement of the soundness of a reasoning, not to pay immediate attention to the truth or falsity of premisses and conclusion. In itself the falsity of the premisses does not affect the soundness of an argument, nor is it guaranteed by the truth of the conclusion.

2. FUNDAMENTAL CRITERION FOR THE SOUNDNESS OF ARGUMENTS

I consider the tracing of general criteria for the soundness of arguments as the fundamental problem of formal logic. The treatment of this problem, however, gives rise to other questions which, for example, concern the doctrine of definitions; these also belong to formal logic.

Now suppose that we want to investigate the soundness of the following arguments:

(I)	(II)
No Mammoth is a Partridge	*Some Partridges are not Mammoths*
All Sheep are Mammoths	*Some Mammoths are not Sheep*
∴ *No Partridge is a Sheep*	∴ *Some Partridges are not Sheep*

We consider then not only both arguments given, but besides these also all arguments which are created by the substitution of:

> *Mammoth* by: *Mouse, Marmot, Mollusk, Monkey, Marabou, Mosquito,* ...;
> *Partridge* by: *Panther, Parrot, Pachyderm, Puma, Polar Bear, Python,* ...;
> *Sheep* by: *Shrimp, Snake, Skunk, Starling, Sparrow, Stork, Snail,* ...;

Of the innumerably many arguments which we can obtain in this manner, I will mention two more by way of example:

(I′)	(II′)
No Mosquito is a Puma	*Some Pythons are not Monkeys*
All Shrimp are Mosquitoes	*Some Monkeys are not Snakes*
∴ *No Puma is a Shrimp*	... *Some Pythons are not Snakes*

The argument under (II′) has a particular property: both premisses are *true*, but the conclusion is *false*. On that basis we now deny soundness not only to the argument under (II′), but also to the argument under (II) and to *all* arguments which can be obtained from these by a similar substitution of terms.

On the other hand, in all the arguments obtained by substitution of terms from the argument under (I), there are none in which the premisses are true but the conclusion false. On this basis we grant soundness to the argument under (I) and to *all* arguments which can be obtained from it by a substitution of terms.

We say that we, by a substitution of the terms *Mammoth, Partridge, Sheep,* by *Monkey, Python, Snake,* obtain a *counterexample* to judge the soundness of the argument under (II). Making use of the concept *counterexample*, we can now formulate *the fundamental criterion for the soundness of arguments* as follows:

> *An argument is sound if and only if it admits no counterexample.*

This criterion was known already to Aristotle, and it has been applied as long as mankind has tried to reason logically. Its fundamental character, however, has been understood only much later. In 1955 I myself have shown how one can construct logic in a very simple and transparent way directly on the basis of the fundamental criterion.[1]

3. THE FORMAL CHARACTER OF LOGIC

Evidently each argument contains certain elements which are *capable of substitution*; these are the *terms*, in our case: *Mammoth, Partridge, Sheep.* Besides these there are the elements which are not changed by the substitution of terms. The elements capable of substitution determine the *content* of the argument, the others are characteristic for its *form*.[2] In the two cases we consider this form can be characterized by the following schemata:

(I°)	(II°)
No M is a P	*Some P's are not M's*
All S's are M's	*Some M's are not S's*
$\therefore$ *No P is an S*	$\therefore$ *Some P's are not S's*

Now the soundness of a given argument is exclusively dependent on its *form*. In other words: if an argument of a given form is sound, then all arguments of that form are sound; if an argument of a given form is not sound, then no argument of that form is sound. In particular all arguments of the form (I°), the modus CELANTES of traditional syllogistics, are sound, while all arguments of the form under (II°) are not sound.

4. THE TRANSITION TO MATHEMATICAL LOGIC

The procedure followed is unsatisfactory to the extent that the search for a counterexample was made haphazardly. If we encounter a suitable counterexample in this manner, then it is thereby once and for all established that arguments of the form considered are not sound. But if we do not immediately encounter a suitable counterexample, then this will in general absolutely not guarantee that arguments of the form considered *are* sound; that would only be the case if the search had been made in a systematic way.

We can say that modern logic is distinguished from the traditional because it enables us to *search for suitable counterexamples in a systematic way*. In an analogous way algebra was a step forward compared to antique arithmetic, because it opened the possibility of a more systematic treatment of certain questions. This is one of the considerations which explains the designation of modern logic as '*mathematical logic*'. This designation could invite critique because it suggests:

(i) That modern logic is constructed according to mathematical example and even according to mathematical principles;

(ij) That modern logic does not want to be (or at least is not) a doctrine of the soundness of arguments in general, but more in particular a doctrine of mathematical argumentation.

With regard to the first point, one can argue that the use of symbols in logic goes back already to Aristotle, so that its usage in logic is just as old as its use in mathematics. In Boëthius[3] we find formulations like:

si, cum est a, est b, cum sit c, est d,

which are strongly reminiscent of formulas like:

$$(a \to b) \to (c \to d)$$

in modern logic. Here already there is a clear tendency to *formalization*.[4] As *variables*, comparable to the $x, y, z, \ldots$ from algebra and with the $A, B, C, \ldots$ from geometry, Boëthius uses the letters $a, b, c, d, \ldots$; as *logical constants* (in our example: as an expression of implication) he apparently uses words (*si* and *cum*). One should meanwhile keep in mind that the more rigorous structure of the classical languages lends itself to such a partial formalization better than the looser sentence structure of the modern languages. One can, I believe, assert freely that the usage of symbols, as well as the formalization possible on the strength of them, is in logic and mathematics based on the same considerations.

The second point presupposes the opinion according to which the argumentation in mathematics has a character different from the one in other areas. This opinion occurs in all kinds of variations, but the most current version goes back to Descartes and Kant; according to them mathematical argumentation always involves an appeal to an *intuitive vision*. We shall see, however, that this opinion has no basis; with that point (ij) also is disposed of.

Nevertheless there is in fact a close connection between modern logic and *mathematical foundational studies*. The explanation of this connection is based on two considerations. In the first place mathematical foundational studies, notably *logicism*, has strongly stimulated the need for logical insight and by that the development of modern logic. Secondly, a modern logic, to be a match for traditional logic, has to satisfy heavy requirements in the way of *rigorousness of construction* and *completeness with respect to subject matter*.

The first requirement will need little illustration. The second requirement means that logic has to enable us to judge arguments of the most divergent character. To be able to test this, we therefore have to have at our disposal a great quantity of arguments, the soundness of which leaves no room for doubt. Such a supply is furnished only by mathematics, and it forms therefore the indicated 'drill-ground' for modern logic.

5. CONSTRUCTION OF A FRAGMENT OF MODERN LOGIC

I now want to sketch the construction of a fragment of modern logic which corresponds to the traditional doctrine of the *assertoric syllogism*.

(1) We will make use of the following symbols:

(i)　　　　Indefinite terms $A, B, C, ..., M, P, S$;

(ij)　　　　Indefinite individual names $a, b, c, ...$;

(iij)　　　Individual variables $x, y, z, ...$;

(iv)　　　The *negation* —, the *conjunction* & and the implication →;

(v)　　　The *universal quantifiers* $(x), (y), (z), ...$ and the *existential quantifiers* $(Ex), (Ey), (Ez), ...$.

(2) Proceeding from these symbols, in the first place we construct *atomic formulas*, $A(a), A(b), A(c), ..., A(x), A(y), ..., B(a), B(b), ..., B(x)$, $..., C(a), ..., M(a), M(b), ..., M(x), ..., P(a), ...$.

(3) Next we form more complicated formulas on the basis of the following rules:

(i)　　　　If U is a formula, then $\bar{U}, (x)\, U, (y)\, U, ..., (Ex)\, U, (Ey)\, U, ...$ are also formulas;

(ij)　　　If U and V are formulas, then $U \& V$ and $U \to V$ are also formulas. [The rules (i) and (ij) are subject to certain restrictions, which I don't choose to go into at the moment.]

(4) In the *interpretation* of the formulas we imagine that a (non-empty) domain **D** of individual objects is given. The terms $A, B, C, ...,$ M, P, S are thought to express predicates which can be applied to the individuals of **D**. The letters $a, b, c, ...$ are considered as names of individuals of **D**, while the variables $x, y, z, ...$ are thought of as ranging over *all* individuals of **D**.

Then $A(a)$ expresses that the predicate A applies to the individual a, $A(x)$ expresses the condition that the predicate A applies to the individual x of **D**. $\bar{U}$ expresses the negation of U, $(x) U$ expresses that each individual x of **D** satisfies the condition U and $(Ex) U$ expresses that at least one individual x of **D** satisfies the condition U. $U \& V$ expresses the simultaneous affirmation of U and V, and $U \rightarrow V$ the affirmation of V under the condition U. –

We now return to the considerations about the soundness of the arguments under (I) and (II). The premisses and the conclusion of the argument under (I) can now be represented by the formulas:

(1) $\overline{(Ex) \; [M(x) \& P(x)]}$,
(2) $\quad (y) \; [S(y) \rightarrow M(y)]$,
(3) $\overline{(Ez) \; [P(z) \& S(z)]}$.

The tableau below can then be considered as a description of a systematic attempt to construct a suitable counterexample.

True		False	
(1) $\overline{(Ex) \; [M(x) \& P(x)]}$		(3) $\overline{(Ez) \; [P(z) \& S(z)]}$	
(2) $\quad (y) \; [S(y) \rightarrow M(y)]$			
(4) $\quad (Ez) \; [P(z) \& S(z)]$ see: (3)		(5) $(Ex) \; [M(x) \& P(x)]$ see: (1)	
(6) $P(a) \& S(a)$,, (4)			
(7) $P(a)$,, (6)			
(8) $S(a)$,, (6)			
(9) $S(a) \rightarrow M(a)$,, (2)		(10) $M(a) \& P(a)$,, (5)	
1	2	[1] (11) $M(a)$ (10)	[2] (12) $P(a)$ (10)
11	[12] (14) $M(a)$ (9)	[11] (13) $S(a)$ (9)	12

The following remarks may serve as a further illustration.

(1)–(3) The placing of these formulas fixes the requirements which any suitable counter-example will have to fulfill.

(4) For formula (3) to be false, this formula must be true.

(5) For formula (1) to be true, this formula must be false.

(6) For formula (4) to be true, **D** has to contain at least one individual, which, taken as the value of z, satisfies the condition $P(z) \& S(z)$; if we denote this individual by a, then formula (6) must be true.

(7)–(8) For formula (6) to be true, both these formulas have to be true.

(9) For formula (2) to be true, each individual of **D** has to fulfill the condition $S(y) \to M(y)$; this in particular holds for the individual we have just called a; thus formula (9) must be true.

(10) For formula (5) to be false, no individual of **D** may fulfill the condition $M(x) \& P(x)$; so this also holds for the individual a, so that formula (10) will have to be false.

(11)–(12) For formula (10) to be false either $M(a)$ or $P(a)$ has to be false. There are therefore two possibilities, and because of that we split our tableau, with the aid of two vertical lines, into two sub-tableaux, [1] and [2], each of which corresponds to one of these two possibilities. – Thus far we only pay attention to formula (10). Now we remark, though, that $P(a)$ cannot be at the same time true as formula (7) and false as formula (12); the possibility suggested by sub-tableau [2] is therefore disposed of, and so this tableau is closed (double horizontal lines).

(13)–(14) We first ask ourselves under which conditions the formula (9) $S(a) \to M(a)$ would be false; evidently this is the case if $S(a)$ is true and $M(a)$ is nevertheless false. The formula $S(a) \to M(a)$ is therefore true, if this double condition is *not* satisfied. There are two possibilities for this: in the first place $S(a)$ can be false and in the second place $M(a)$ can be true. So we split the remaining sub-tableau [1] into two sub-tableaux [11] and [12], which each represent one possibility. – Thus far, however, we have only paid attention to formula (9); if we also take into account the formulas (8) and (11), then it is evident that both sub-tableaux [11] and [12] are closed.

Our systematic attempt to construct a suitable counterexample has therefore failed. So there *cannot* be a suitable counterexample, and thus on the basis of our fundamental criterion the soundness of the argument under (I) has definitively been established.

For the argument under (II) we obtain the following tableau.

True		False	
(1) $(Ex)\,[P(x)\,\&\,\overline{M(x)}]$		(3) $(Ez)\,[P(z)\,\&\,\overline{S(z)}]$	
(2) $(Ey)\,[M(y)\,\&\,\overline{S(y)}]$			
(4) $P(a)\,\&\,\overline{M(a)}$	(1)		
(5) $P(a)$	(4)		
(6) $\overline{M(a)}$	(4)		
(7) $M(b)\,\&\,\overline{S(b)}$	(2)		
(8) $M(b)$	(7)		
(9) $\overline{S(b)}$	(7)	(10) $P(a)\,\&\,\overline{S(a)}$	(3)
^{1}	^{2}	^{1} (11) $P(a)$ (10)	^{2} (12) $\overline{S(a)}$ (10)
(13) $S(a)$	(12)	(14) $P(b)\,\&\,\overline{S(b)}$	(3)
^{21}	^{22}	^{21} (15) $P(b)$ (14)	^{22} (16) $\overline{S(b)}$ (14)
		(17) $M(a)$ (6)	
		(18) $S(b)$	(9)

In this case the construction is completed without the tableau being 'closed'. We can now read off from the tableau a suitable counterexample. The domain **D** has to contain two individuals a and b, while the formulas $P(a)$, $S(a)$, and $M(b)$ have to be true and the formulas $M(a)$, $P(b)$ and $S(b)$ false.

Both of the tableaux considered have, apart from complications yet to be discussed, paradigmatic significance. If one is asked about the soundness of an argument which, starting from certain premises U_1, U_2, ..., U_m, yields a certain conclusion V, then we can always construct a *semantic tableau* in analogous way. The construction can only yield two results:

(I) The tableau is '*closed*'. This means that a systematic attempt (and therefore *every* attempt) to construct a suitable counterexample fails. There *is* therefore no counterexample, and so, indeed, the conclusion V follows logically from the premises U_1, U_2, ..., U_m.

(II) The tableau is not closed. In that case the tableau itself delivers a suitable counterexample as a proof that the argument in question cannot be sound.

6. NATURAL DEDUCTION

An argument which, proceeding from the premisses $U_1, U_2, ..., U_m$, yields the conclusion V, can be sound, therefore, if and only if the corresponding semantic tableau closes. On the other hand, now let the premisses $U_1, U_2, ..., U_m$ and the conclusion V be chosen in such a way that the corresponding semantic tableau closes. Then V follows logically from $U_1, U_2, ..., U_m$ and so we expect that it will be possible to construct an argument from which this is apparent.

Now we could once and for all declare any closed semantic tableau to be an argument. The objection arises, however, that such a tableau does not have the usual form of an argument which 'proceeds' from the premisses given and finally 'yields' the desired conclusion. Meanwhile it is not difficult to remedy this defect. Consider the closed tableau of page 14:

(1)	$(Ex)\,[M\,(x)\,\&\,P\,(x)]$	[prem 1]
(2)	$(y)\,[S\,(y)\to M\,(y)]$	[prem 2]
----	--------------------------------	------------
(4)	$(Ez)\,[P\,(z)\,\&\,S\,(z)]$	[+ hyp 1]
....	....	....
(6)	$P\,(a)\,\&\,S\,(a)$	[+ hyp 2]
(7)	$P\,(a)$	(6)
(8)	$S\,(a)$	(6)
(9)	$S\,(a)\to M\,(a)$	(2)
(14)	$M\,(a)$	(8), (9)
(10)	$M\,(a)\,\&\,P\,(a)$	(14), (7)
....	....	....
(5)	$(Ex)\,[M\,(x)\,\&\,P\,(x)]$	[− hyp 2]
----	--------------------------------	------------
(3)	$(Ez)\,[P\,(z)\,\&\,S\,(z)]$	[− hyp 1]

By a simple realignment of the formulas in the tableau we get an argument which would fit into what G. Gentzen[5] has denoted as a *calculus of natural deduction*. I want to clarify this argument somewhat more.

(1)–(2) We start from the premisses given.

(4)–(6) We introduce two hypotheses, which will afterwards be eliminated. The part of the argument 'taxed' with such an hypothesis is marked by means of horizontal lines.

(7)–(8) These formulas very clearly follow from formula (6).

(9) We apply premiss (2) to the individual a.

(14) We apply *modus ponens* to the formulas (8) and (9).*

(10) This formula follows from formulas (14) and (7).

(5) This formula follows from formula (10). It does not depend, however, on hypothesis 2; it is valid on the condition that there exists at least one individual which satisfies the condition $P(z) \& S(z)$, but it does not matter that we have called this individual a.

(3) Formula (5) is contradictory to premiss 1. We hold hypothesis 1 responsible for this contradiction. We therefore reject this hypothesis, which is thereby at the same time eliminated.

7. SUPPLEMENTARY CONSIDERATIONS

The line of thought developed in par. 1–6 will be worked out more in detail in Chapters II–IV. To conclude this chapter, I therefore would like to mention some supplementary considerations which indicate that we cannot be content with the rough exposition given here, and will have to go deeper into a number of points.

(1) It occurs that we can justify a conclusion without having to appeal to one or more premisses. As an example I mention *Plato's law*,

$$(Ex) [(Ey) A (y) \to A(x)],$$

or, in words:

> There is an object with the peculiarity that, if there exists one object with the property A, then the first object has to possess the property A.

To recognize the validity of this law, we consider the semantic tableau:

True		False	
		(1) $(Ex) [(Ey) A(y) \to A(x)]$	
		(2) $(Ey) A(y) \to A(a)$	(1)
(3) $(Ey) A(y)$	(2)	(4) $A(a)$	(2)
(5) $A(b)$	(3)	(6) $(Ey) A(y) \to A(b)$	(1)
(7) $(Ey) A(y)$	(6)	(8) $A(b)$	(6)

From this closed tableau it is evident that the formula considered can never be false, and therefore is always true. Formulas with this property are designated as *logical laws,* as *logical identities,* as *logical truths,* or as *tautologies.* I will return to the question whether this kind of formula indeed deserves the contempt which is expressed in the last denomination.

(2) The conversion of a closed semantic tableau into a natural deduction does not always go as smoothly as in the particular case chosen as an example in par. 6.

Already the semantic tableau we have just constructed for Plato's law presents an example of the difficulties which can arise in this connection. Chapter III will be mainly devoted to surmounting these difficulties.

(3) The construction of a semantic tableau can lead to a *regressus in infinitum.* This is related to the circumstance that we, contrary to traditional logic, also have to reckon with the occurrence of *binary predicates* or *relations.*

We obtain a simple example if we ask the question whether the conclusion $(Ez)(t) A(t, z)$ is derivable from the premiss $(x) (Ey) A(x, y)$.

True		False	
(1) $(x) (Ey) A(x, y)$		(2) $(Ez) (t) A(t, z)$	
(3) $(Ey) A(a, y)$	(1)	(4) $(t) A(t, a)$	(2)
(5) $A(a, b)$	(3)	(6) $A(c, a)$	(4)
(7) $(Ey) A(b, y)$	(1)	(9) $(t) A(t, b)$	(2)
(8) $(Ey) A(c, y)$	(1)	(10) $(t) A(t, c)$	(2)
(11) $A(b, d)$	(7)	(13) $A(f, b)$	(9)
(12) $A(c, e)$	(8)	(14) $A(g, c)$	(10)
.		.	
.		.	
.		.	

In this case the course of the construction is even more easily surveyed, and therefore it is not difficult to read off the tableau a counterexample as a proof of the fact that the deduction in question is not possible. But at the same time it is clear that in other cases we have to be prepared for all kinds of complications.

NOTES

[1] E. W. Beth [79].

[2] We say that two arguments have the *same form* if each of the two can be obtained from the other by a suitable substitution of terms.

[3] K. Dürr [1], [2].

[4] That one was fully aware of this tendency, even in antiquity, is, for example, clear from a statement of Theophrastus, reproduced in I. M. Bocheński [1] p. 157, 24.08.

[5] G. Gentzen [1].

* *Annotation.* See page 22.

CHAPTER II

INFERENTIAL AND CLASSICAL LOGIC

8. SEMANTIC AND OPERATIONAL ASPECTS OF MEANING

An often heard grievance against mathematical logic is based on the supposed presence of conventional, artificial, arbitrary and accidental elements. This grievance feeds on the fact that the formalists and their successors (like H. B. Curry[1] and P. Lorenzen[2]) defend a view according to which the logical symbols have no actual meaning, or at least the meaning of the logical symbols is not relevant for logic. Opposing this view is the endeavor of a scholar like H. Scholz[3], to found logic on the meaning of the logical symbols. Is perhaps a standpoint possible with more nuances than the dilemma seemingly urged on us here?

Wittgenstein's slogan: "Don't ask for the meaning, ask for the use"[4], is, in my opinion, much more acceptable if we give to it the following very free explanation. What is commonly denoted by the pre-scientific term 'meaning' has at least two aspects: (1) the *naming of* or *reference to* a matter by means of a word or symbol, and (2) the *usage* of that word or symbol in an appropriate context.

Now it is often difficult to sustain in practice the distinction between the *semantic* and the *operational* aspects of meaning, because with respect to words of ordinary language these aspects are so closely bound. In the construction of formalized languages, on the other hand, where we can stipulate the meaning of the symbols arbitrarily within wide boundaries, we have the opportunity to place by choice the operational or the semantic aspect in the spotlight.

9. PURELY IMPLICATIONAL LOGIC

I want now to demonstrate this possibility on the basis of a construction of a very rudimentary fragment of logic, *purely implicational logic*.

The *formulas* of this theory are characterized by means of the following stipulations:

(F 1)   All atoms $A, B, C, \ldots$ are formulas;

(F 2)   If U and V are formulas, $U \rightarrow V$ is also a formula;

(F 3)   Nothing shall be a formula, except on the strength of (F 1) and (F 2).

We will denote arbitrary formulas by $U, V, W, X, Y, Z, \ldots$; we denote sets of formulas by $K, K', K'', \ldots$; $L, L', L'', \ldots$; we will sometimes mention the empty set, which is denoted by $\emptyset$.

10. DEDUCTION PROBLEMS AND DEDUCTIVE TABLEAUX

In establishing the *meaning* of the formulas considered, we take, to start with, an operational point of view. A formula $U \rightarrow V$ has to represent a proposition: '*If U, then V*'. The meaning of such a proposition is operationally characterized by the *modus ponens*:

$$\frac{\begin{array}{l} \textit{If } U,\textit{ then } V \\ \qquad U \end{array}}{\therefore \quad V}$$

The meaning of a formula $U \rightarrow V$ will also be operationally characterized by the way in which such a formula can be manipulated in the context of a logical argument.

We therefore introduce *sequents K/Z*, or

Premisses	Conclusion
K	Z

, i.e.

Premisses	Conclusion
U_1	Z
U_2	
.	
.	
.	
U_m	

Such a sequent expresses a *deduction problem*, namely the question if and how, proceeding from the premisses K or $(U_1, U_2, \ldots, U_m)$, the conclusion Z can be derived. Should the answer to this question be affirmative, then we will consider the sequent K/Z as *valid*.

   a. If the formula $U \rightarrow V$ occurs among the premisses K, then it is clear how we will be able to profit from this premiss. We first try to derive the conclusion U from the premisses K. If that is successful, then we apply *modus ponens* to $U \rightarrow V$ and U. We add the conclusion V, thus obtained, to the premisses K, and we now try to derive the conclusion Z from the premisses (K, V).

The reduction schema:

	Premisses			Conclusion	
	K'			Z	
	$U \rightarrow V$				
(ij^a)					
	1	2	1		2
		V	U		Z

shows how, on the basis of this consideration, the original deduction problem:

$$(K', U \rightarrow V)/Z$$

has been reduced to two deduction problems:

[1] $(K', U \rightarrow V)/U$,
[2] $(K', U \rightarrow V, V)/Z$

b. Now let $U \rightarrow V$ be the conclusion sought from the premisses K. We consider that $U \rightarrow V$ is *completely* characterized by the *modus ponens*, in the sense that $U \rightarrow V$ can *only* serve in combination with U to yield the conclusion V. Then the derivability of $U \rightarrow V$ from K stands or falls with the derivability of V from (K, U). This insight yields the reduction schema:

	Premisses	Conclusion
	K	$U \rightarrow V$
(ij^b)		
	U	V

c. If the desired conclusion Z occurs among the premisses K, then the deduction asked for by the sequent K/Z is always feasible; this insight yields the *closure schema:*

	Premisses	Conclusion
	K'	Z
	Z	
(i)		

As an example we consider the deduction problem:

$$(A \to B, B \to C)/A \to C.$$

The consecutive reductions of this problem are, with the applications of the closure scheme, rendered in the form of a *deductive tableau.*

	Premisses		Conclusion	
	(1) $A \to B$		(3) $A \to C$	
	(2) $B \to C$			
(ij^b)				
	(4) A		(5) C	
(ij^a)				
	1	2	1	2
		(7) B	(6) A	(5) C
(i)				
(ij^a)				
	21	22	21	22
		(9) C	(8) B	(5) C
(i)				

The presence of formula (3) gives rise to the application of reduction schema (ij^b), by which the problem posed is reduced to:

$$(A \to B, B \to C, A)/C.$$

The presence of formula (1), by the application of reduction schema (ij^a), enables the reduction of this problem to the two problems:

[1] $(A \to B, B \to C, A)/A,$
[2] $(A \to B, B \to C, A, B)/C,$

the first one of which can be solved, so that we can apply the closure schema. Subsequently, on the strength of the presence of formula (2), we once more apply reduction schema (ij^a), by which deduction problem [2] is reduced to:

[21] $(A \to B, B \to C, A, B)/B,$
[22] $(A \to B, B \to C, A, B, C)/C,$

both of which can be solved. The problem is thereby reduced to problems which can be solved and therefore can itself also be solved. The deduction of the conclusion $A \to C$ from the premisses can be represented as follows.

$$
\begin{array}{clll}
& (1) & A \to B & [\text{prem}] \\
& (2) & B \to C & [\text{prem}] \\
& & \text{-------} & \\
& (4) & A & [+\text{hyp } 1] \\
[\ 1] \quad [(6) & A & (4) \\
(7) & B & (1), (6) \\
[21] \quad [(8) & B & (7) \\
[22] \quad [(9) & C & (2), (8) \\
[2] \qquad (5) & C & (9) \\
(5) & C & (5) \\
(5) & C & (5) \\
& & \text{-------} & \\
(3) & A \to C & [-\text{hyp } 1]
\end{array}
$$

The applications of reduction shema (ij^a), as could be expected, show up as applications of *modus ponens*. The application of reduction schema (ij^b) now takes the form of a 'reverse *modus ponens*'. We first add formula (4) as a hypothesis to the premisses (1) and (2). Thereby we are enabled to derive formula (5). Next we take the hypothesis back, and thus obtain the desired conclusion as formula (3).

11. TRUTH-VALUE PROBLEMS AND SEMANTIC TABLEAUX

We now take a semantic point of view and give the following stipulations concerning the application of '*truth-values*' to our formulas.

(S 1)   The truth-value of each of the atoms $A, B, C, \ldots$ can arbitrarily be assigned as *true* or *false*;

(S 2) $U \to V$ is *true*, if U is *false* or V *true*; $U \to V$ is *false*, if U is *true* and V *false*.

We now introduce sequents K/L, or

True	False		True	False
K	L		U_1	V_1
			U_2	V_2
			.	.
			.	.
			.	.
			U_m	V_n

Such a sequent expresses a *truth-value problem*: is it possible to assign the truth-values of the atoms A, B, C,... in such a way that all formulas in K, or $(U_1, U_2,... U_m)$, become *true*, and all formulas in L, or $(V_1, V_2,..., V_n)$ become *false*? If the answer to this question is negative, then we will designate the sequent K/L as *valid*. If the sequent K/Z is valid, then we consider Z as *logical consequence* of K.

For truth-value problems as described here, apparently the following *closure* and *reduction schemata* hold:

	True	False
	K'	L'
	Z	Z
(i)		

	True		False				True	False
	K'		L				K	L'
	$U \to V$							$U \to V$
(ijᵃ)						(ijᵇ)		
	1	2	1	2				
		V	U				U	V

12. INFERENTIAL AND CLASSICAL LOGIC – PEIRCE'S LAW

Although there is a striking resemblance between the schemata for deduction problems and those for truth-value problems, they are not equivalent. This becomes clear if we apply them to the following sequent:

$$\emptyset/[(A \to B) \to A] \to A.$$

We then obtain the following tableaux:

	Premisses		Conclusion	
(ij^b)			(1) [...] → A	
(ij^a)	(2) (...) → A		(3) A	
	1	2	1	2
(i)	......	(5) A	(4) A → B	(3) A
(ij^b)			....	
(ij^a)	(6) A		(7) B	
	11	12	11	12
(ij^b)		(9) A	(8) A → B	(7) B
	(10) A	....	(11) B	

	True	False	
(ij^b)		(1) [...] → A	
(ij^a)	(2) (...) → A	(3) A	
	1	2	1	2
(i)	......	(5) A	(4) A → B	
(ij^b)		....	
(i)	(6) A	(7) B	

The semantic tableau [bottom] is closed, which is not the case with the deductive tableau [top]. Although in the sense of the semantics the formula $[(A \to B) \to A] \to A$ *follows logically* from the empty set of premisses $\emptyset$, this formula is *not derivable* from the empty set of premisses $\emptyset$ on the basis of an operational construction of logic.

Accordingly, as we take an operational or a semantic point of view, we apparently obtain different systems. This does not hold only on the level of pure implicational logic; the line of thought sketched here can be extended to the whole area of elementary logic. It turns out that from an operational standpoint one comes to *inferential* (or *intuitionistic*) *logic*,

while *two-valued* (or *classical*) *logic* obviously corresponds to the semantic standpoint.

Curiously enough in extending *purely implicational logic* to *elementary
logic* no new divergencies between inferential and two-valued logic
emerge. In fact, if we add to inferential logic axiomatically all formulas:

$$[(U \rightarrow V) \rightarrow U] \rightarrow U$$

then we obtain classical logic. That is to say: let K/Z be a sequent which is
valid classically, but not inferentially; then by supplementing K with
suitably chosen formulas $[(U \rightarrow V) \rightarrow U] \rightarrow U$, one can obtain a premiss
set K^+ such that the sequent K^+/Z is also inferentially valid.

The acceptance of *Peirce's Law* which asserts the correctness of all
formulas:

$$[(U \rightarrow V) \rightarrow U] \rightarrow U$$

thus determines the transition from inferential to classical logic.

The difference between these two systems is therefore, on the level of
purely implicational logic, already completely present.

13. OTHER ASPECTS OF MEANING

I have proceeded in this chapter from the thought that *'meaning'* in the
pre-scientific sense possesses at least two aspects which I respectively
denoted as the *semantic* and the *operational*. Taking these two aspects
into account, we get an insight into the curious fact that there are two
'natural' systems of formal logic which one respectively calls *classical*
and *inferential logic*.

Other more or less comparable aspects of *'meaning'* have not been
taken into account. There are, for that matter, no indications that these
aspects would be of any importance for the construction of formal logic.

Of course one can observe that I have exclusively discussed extremely
simple language forms. One will not be able, however, to derive a rightful
argument against the results obtained from this observation. The concentration on these two aspects of meaning just brought about the
advantage that the influence of these aspects on logic could be demonstrated clearly and unambiguously.

Some of the aspects of meaning which we did not consider have, for that matter, been investigated with regard to problems concerning the foundation and construction of logic. I am thinking here of Frege's distinction between '*Sinn*' and '*Bedeutung*', of Mannoury's distinction between *speak-* and *hear-meaning* and between *indicative, emotional,* and *volitional elements of meaning,* and Morris's distinction between *syntax, semantics and pragmatics.* In this connection, especially, the recent work of R. M. Martin[5] should also be mentioned.

14. INFORMAL LOGIC: G. MANNOURY, A. NAESS, CH. PERELMAN

A deeper investigation into the aspects of meaning mentioned in par. 13 would be very important in connection with the rather numerous studies about the area one could designate as *informal logic.*

It very often happens that somebody tries to convince his audience by means of arguments which cannot be considered sound from the standpoint of formal logic. In some cases this is a question of conscious or unconscious deception, but that is by no means always the case. In certain situations logically unsound arguments are nevertheless considered convincing.

Ch. Perelman[6] has pointed out that such informal arguments are also judged according to definite established rules, so that in this connection one can speak of figures of argumentation. In further investigations in this direction one will undoubtedly be able to use to his advantage the work of G. Mannoury and A. Naess.

NOTES

[1] H. B. Curry [1].
[2] P. Lorenzen [1].
[3] H. Scholz and G. Hasenjaeger [1].
[4] L. Linsky [1].
[5] R. M. Martin [1].
[6] Ch. Perelman and L. Olbrechts-Tyteca [1].

CHAPTER III

PROOF BY CONTRADICTION

15. INTRODUCTORY REMARKS

Besides the subject mentioned in the title, we will bring also another theme up for discussion in this chapter, namely, the systematic conversion of closed deductive and semantic tableaux, already alluded to in par. 7.

According to widespread opinion a proof by contradiction, except in those cases where it is the intention to justify a negative conclusion, is not as valuable as a direct proof. Often one demands that even there where a proof by contradiction is almost urged onto one, this is afterwards nevertheless converted into a direct proof.[1]

In this chapter we will try to determine how it is possible that even with an affirmative conclusion a proof by contradiction is sometimes the most obvious, and that the conversion of such a proof into a direct argumentation in that case often gives very great difficulties. Here I have mainly the argumentation on the basis of classical logic in mind.

The framework of my argument can be described as follows. A suitable starting point for the construction of formal logic lies in the construction of semantic tableaux. If such a semantic tableau closes, then the conclusion under consideration follows logically from the premisses given. In par. 7 we could give to such a closed semantic tableau the more common form of an argument which 'proceeds' from the premisses and finally 'yields' the desired conclusion. In par. 16 we will see, however, that such a conversion in other cases will not directly succeed.

We now further remark that, as can be expected, the conversion of a closed deductive tableau into a natural deduction never leads to difficulties. The difficulties which can occur in the conversion of a semantic tableau will therefore be tackled in such a way that we will first try to convert the semantic tableau in question into a deductive tableau, which subsequently can be converted into a natural deduction; for the first conversion a trick is required. We have the choice though between several equivalent tricks; the most obvious trick yields a deductive tableau, the conversion of which turns out to lead to a proof by contradiction.

16. CONVERSION OF CLOSED TABLEAUX
INTO NATURAL DEDUCTIONS

The conversion of the deductive tableau in par. 10 and of the semantic tableau in par. 7 did not present any difficulties. We now consider, however, the closed semantic tableaux for the sequents:

$$\emptyset/[(A \to B) \to A] \to A$$

(par. 12) and:

$$\emptyset/(Ex)\,[(Ey)\,A\,(y) \to A\,(x)]$$

(par. 7).

The first tableau yields the following sequence of formulas:

(2)	$(A \to B) \to A$	$[+\,\text{hyp } 1]$
(6)	A	$[+\,\text{hyp } 2]$
(7)	B	$[?\,?\,?]$
(4)	$A \to B$	$[-\,\text{hyp } 2]$
(3)	A	$(2),\,(4)$
(1)	$[(A \to B) \to A] \to A$	$[-\,\text{hyp } 1]$

The second tableau yields a sequence of formulas in which one can find only very little logical connection. The sequence above, however, would be acceptable as a deduction if we could give an acceptable explanation of the occurrence of formula (7). Such an explanation is in any case not obvious. In the deductive tableau in par. 12 subtableau [1] does not close because the premisses (2) and (6) do not yield formula (7) as a conclusion. In the corresponding semantic tableau, subtableau [1] does close, but that is because of the co-occurrence of formulas (6) and (3). In the deductive tableau this co-occurrence does not lead to closure, as formula (6) only occurs after formula (3) has been supplanted by formula (7). And the possibility of always converting a closed deductive tableau into a natural deduction is based, on the other hand, on the fact that a formula in the right hand column of a deductive tableau is "*supplanted*" by later occurring formulas.

To be able to convert a closed semantic tableau into a natural deduction all the time, we apparently have to take care that in such a tableau a similar 'supplanting' takes place. On the other hand, however, we have to prevent this 'supplanting' from forming an obstacle to a possible closure of certain subtableaux. Therefore we will have to 'store' a formula which is being 'supplanted' in some way or another (and that is, of course, only possible in the left-hand column) in such a way that we can 'restore' the supplanted formula to the right hand column later, if so desired.

17. THE NEGATION

To be able to take into account reasoning in which also the negation plays a role we add to the rule (F 1–3) in par. 9 the following clause:

(F 2^a)   If U is a formula, then $\bar{U}$ is also a formula, and we state the following semantical rule:

(S 3) $\bar{U}$ is *true* if U is *false*; $\bar{U}$ is *false* if U is *true*.

To this semantical rule the *following reduction schemata* clearly correspond:

	True	False			True	False
	K'	L			K	L'
	$\bar{U}$					$\bar{U}$
(iij^a)				(iij^b)		
		U			U	

which we will also sustain for deductive tableaux.*

On the basis of the semantic rule (S 3), however, the following (improper) reduction schema will also be justified:

	True	False
	K	L'
		U
(iij^c)		
	$\bar{U}$	U

Together with schema (iij^a), schema (iij^c) now yields the trick which was deemed necessary in par. 15 and par. 16. If U is the formula in the right hand column which threatens to be 'supplanted', then schema (iij^c) yields formula $\bar{U}$ in the left hand column. The 'supplanting' of formula U can no longer make mischief, because schema (iij^a) enables us to 'restore' this formula to the right hand column whenever that is necessary.

18. SEMANTIC AND DEDUCTIVE TABLEAUX

As a final test we consider once again the two sequents mentioned in par. 16. In the semantic tableau for the first sequent formula (3) was supplanted. Supplementation with the corresponding applications of the schemata (iij^a) and (iij^c) yields the semantic tableau:

	True		False	
(ij^b)			(1) $[(A \to B) \to A] \to A$	
(iij^c)	(2) $(A \to B) \to A$		(3) A	
(ij^a)	(3') $\bar{A}$		(3) A	
	1	2	1	2
(i)		(5) A	(4) $A \to B$	(3) A
(ij^b)				
(iij^a)	(6) A		(7) B	
(i)			(3″) A	

The conversion to a natural deduction no longer presents any difficulties; it leads to the following result:

(2)	$(A \to B) \to A$	[+ hyp 1]
(3')	$\bar{A}$	[+ hyp 2]
(6)	A	[+ hyp 3]
(3″)	A	(6)

(7)	B	(3'), (3")

. . . .

(4)	$A \to B$	$[-\text{hyp } 3]$
(5)	A	(4), (2)

_____

(3)	A	$[-\text{hyp } 2]$

- - - - - - - - - - - - -

(1)	$[(A \to B) \to A] \to A$	$[-\text{hyp } 1]$

In the semantic tableau for the second sequent formula (1) was supplanted. By supplementation we now obtain:**

	True		False	
		(1)	$(Ex)\,[(Ey)\,A\,(y) \to A\,(x)]$	
(iij^c)				
	(1') $(Ex)\,[(Ey)\,A\,(y) \to A\,(x)]$	(2)	$(Ey)\,A\,(y) \to A\,(a)$	
	(3) $(Ey)\,A\,(y)$	(4)	$A\,(a)$	
(iij^a)	(5) $A\,(b)$			
		(1")	$(Ex)\,[(Ey)\,A\,(y) \to A\,(x)]$	
		(6)	$(Ey)\,A\,(y) \to A\,(b)$	
	(7) $(Ey)\,A\,(y)$	(8)	$A\,(b)$	

and subsequently by conversion:

- - - - - - - - - - - - - - - -

(1')	$(Ex)\,[(Ey)\,A\,(y) \to A\,(x)]$	$[+\text{hyp } 1]$
(3)	$(Ey)\,A\,(y)$	$[+\text{hyp } 2]$

. . . .

(5)	$A\,(b)$	$[+\text{hyp } 3]$

= = = = = = = = = =

(7)	$(Ey)\,A\,(y)$	$[+\text{hyp } 4]$
(8)	$A\,(b)$	(5)

= = = = = = = = = =

(6)	$(Ey)\,A\,(y) \to A\,(b)$	$[-\text{hyp } 4]$

. . . .

(1")	$(Ex)\,[(Ey)\,A\,(y) \to A\,(x)]$	$[-\text{hyp } 3]$
(4)	$A\,(a)$	(1'), (1")

_____

(2) $(Ey) A(y) \rightarrow A(a)$ $[- \text{hyp } 2]$

- - - - - - - - - - - - - - - -

(1) $(Ex) [(Ey) A(y) \rightarrow A(x)]$ $(- \text{hyp } 1]$

Both reasonings are fully worthy of deeper consideration. In the first place it immediately strikes the eye that we introduce the mutually contradictory hypotheses $\bar{A}$ and A, the one almost immediately after the other. Against this step even moral objections can arise; to soothe the reader I observe that these formulas are in no way affirmed, but are only put forward for discussion, and for the remainder I refer to what I have said already in par. 1.

I also foresee, however, an objection of a more logical nature; the reader will have the tendency to say: 'But in this manner one will be able to prove *everything*!' This observation is completely pertinent. We employ the hypotheses introduced in the conclusion of formula (7), which initially seemed to encounter so many difficulties. We appeal here to a principle already known to traditional logic, as is apparent from the adage: '*Ex falso sequitur quodlibet*' [from falsehoods anything is derivable]. The conclusion B has indeed very little value, because it remains 'taxed' with the hypotheses A and $\bar{A}$.

Once we have obtained the conclusion B, we have to eliminate the hypotheses introduced, according to a general rule beginning with the last. With the hypothesis A this succeeds in the manner we know already from par. 10. Next we find in formula (5) our A again, but now as a conclusion. For this conclusion we hold hypothesis $\bar{A}$ responsible, so that this hypothesis has been taken '*ad absurdum*'. Thereby this hypothesis is also eliminated, so that in formula (3) we come once again to the conclusion A which by this time, however, is only 'taxed' with the hypothesis $(A \rightarrow B) \rightarrow A$. According to the above rule this hypothesis, which was introduced first, will be the last to be eliminated. With horizontal lines (dotted, broken and unbroken) we mark each time that part of the argument which is taxed with a certain hypothesis.

This manner of demarcation is also found in the second argument. Here we appeal to the principle '*Ex falso sequitur quodlibet*' to reach the conclusion $A(a)$. In this case it looks like we have been a little more restrained in the introduction of hypotheses, but that is only seemingly so. Indeed, according to the results of the argument formula (1') can *never* be *true*. A formula with this property is very appropriately designated as a *logical contradiction*. Formula (1) is finally obtained because we have taken the formula (1′) as an hypothesis *ad absurdum* and thereby eliminated it.

A few words about the elimination of hypothesis 3. It is true that formula (1′) is a consequence of formula (6), the derivation of which is taxed with hypothesis 3. Hypothesis 3 and formula (6), however, depend on *b*, which is not the case with formula (1″). Because for formula (1″) the *b* no longer matters, the role of hypothesis 3 with regard to this formula can be taken over by hypothesis 2. In Chapter IV we shall consider this question in a wider context.

To avoid confusion, in closing this section I want to review once more the deduction methods considered thus far (we won't make an appeal to any others); they are:

  a. the closed deductive tableau;

  b. the natural deduction obtained by the conversion of a closed deductive tableau;

  c. the closed semantic tableau;

  d. the closed semantic tableau, supplemented in the way indicated above here;

  e. the natural deduction obtained by the supplementation and conversion of a closed semantic tableau.

The methods under a. and b. are mutually equivalent. They are in summary designated as *intuitionistic logic*; this system comes up for discussion here only in so far as it is important for the following.

The methods under c.–e. are also mutually equivalent. They are in summary designated as *classical* (or *two-valued*) *logic* and present the actual theme of our considerations.

Classical logic is *stronger* than inferential logic in the following sense. Every deduction which is inferentially possible is also classically possible. The deductions corresponding to the sequent:

$$\emptyset/[(A \to B) \to A] \to A$$

(*Pierce's law*), and to the sequent:

$$\emptyset/(Ex)\,[(Ey)\,A\,(y) \to A\,(x)]$$

(*Plato's law*), are classically but *not* inferentially feasible.

19. FINAL CONSIDERATIONS – COMPLETENESS OF CLASSICAL PURELY IMPLICATIONAL LOGIC

As I have indicated already before the trick discussed in par. 17 and par. 18 is indeed the most simple one, but not the only trick which leads to the desired result. On the basis of the semantical rule (S 2), the introduction of the following improper reduction schema is justified:

	True	False
	K	L'
		U
(ij^c)		
	$U \to V$	U

The effectiveness of this trick is clear by comparing two fragments of a semantic tableau.

	True	False			True	False
	K	L			K	L
	·	·			·	·
	·	·			·	·
	·	·			·	·
		U				U
			(ij^c)			
					$U \to V$	
	·	·			·	·
	·	·			·	·
	·	·			·	·
	U	V			U	V

(i)

(ij^a)

	1	2	1	2
		V	U	

(i)

Natural deduction on the basis of *classical purely implicational logic* is characterized by the following *deduction schemata*, each corresponding to the similarly numbered reduction schema:

(i)	(ij^a)	(ij^b)	(ij^c)
K'	K'	K	K
		$\cdots\cdots\cdots\cdots$	$\cdots\cdots\cdots\cdots$
Z	$U \to V,\ U$	U	$U \to V$
Z	V	V	U
		$\cdots\cdots\cdots\cdots$	$\cdots\cdots\cdots\cdots$
		$U \to V$	U

On the strength of deduction schema (i), the conclusion Z is deducible from the premiss set (K', Z), and on the strength of deduction schema (ij^a) [*modus ponens*] the conclusion V is deducible from the premiss set $(K', U \to V, U)$. According to deduction schema (ij^b), for each deduction of V from (K, U) there corresponds a deduction of $U \to V$ from K, and according to deduction schema (ij^c), for each deduction of U from $(K, U \to V)$ there corresponds a deduction of U from K.***

In par. 11 we have designated the sequent K/Z as *valid*, and the conclusion Z as a *logical consequence* of the premiss set K, if for each choice of the truth-values of the atoms $A, B, C, \ldots$ for which all premisses in K become *true*, the conclusion Z also is *true*.

The *completeness* of classical purely implicational logic now finds expression in:

THEOREM 1. If the sequent K/Z is valid, then there is a classical argument which proceeds from the premiss set K and which yields the conclusion Z.

The *proof* of this theorem is actually already implied in the discussion up until now. The arguments, however, are scattered over a lengthy exposition so that a more conveniently arranged formulation does not seem undesirable. We reduce theorem 1 to two lemmas.

By way of introduction we consider the semantic tableau for the sequent:

$$\emptyset/[(A \to B) \to B] \to A$$

True		False	
(2) $(A \to B) \to B$		(1) $[(A \to B) \to B] \to A$ (3) A	
1	2	1	2
(6) A	(5) B	(4) $A \to B$ (7) B	

Subtableau [2] does not close, so that also the tableau as a whole cannot be closed. Now subtableau [2] for the atoms A and B, and thereby also for the other occurring formulas, yields the truth-values mentioned again in a different and more conveniently arranged way in the table below.

A	B	$A \to B$	$(A \to B) \to B$	$[...] \to A$
F	T	T	T	F

The construction of a semantic tableau for a sequent K/L is a *systematic* attempt to choose the truth-values for the atoms A, B, C, ... in such a way that all formulas in K become *true* and at the same time all formulas in L become *false*. This systematic character of the construction has *two* aspects, both of which have to be kept in mind. If the semantic tableau closes, then it is clear from that that the desired choice of the truth-values is not possible; we have designated in that case the sequent K/L as valid.

If the semantic tableau does not close, then it is not only clear from that that a suitable choice of the truth-values in question should be possible, but moreover that each not-closed subtableau yields a set of truth-values as desired.

LEMMA 2. If the sequent K/Z is valid, then the semantic tableau for this sequent is closed.

Proof. The construction of a semantic tableau is a systematic attempt to choose the truth-values of the atoms A, B, C, ... in such a way that all formulas in K become *true*, while the formula Z becomes *false*.

Suppose now that the tableau does not close. We have just seen that then the tableau will yield a suitable set of truth-values. Since according to hypothesis the sequent K/Z is valid, such a set of truth-values cannot exist, however; so the tableau has to close.

LEMMA 3. If the semantic tableau for the sequent K/Z is closed, then there is a classical argument as described in theorem 1.

Proof. We investigate if there occur supplantings in the semantic tableau which in a deductive tableau would have obstructed the closure; for each such supplanting we make an appeal to reduction schema (ij^c). By conversion of the thus supplemented semantic tableau, we subsequently obtain the desired argument.

It is clear that theorem 1 is an immediate consequence of the lemmas 2 and 3. From theorem 1 the following inverse moreover holds:

THEOREM 4. If there is a classical argument which proceeds from the premiss set K and yields the conclusion Z, then the sequent K/Z is valid.

Beforehand we again prove two lemmas.

LEMMA 5. The sequents $(K', Z)/Z$ and $(K', U \rightarrow V, U)/V$ are valid.

Proof. Only the second case has to be considered in more detail. So suppose that all formulas in $(K', U \rightarrow V, U)$, in particular also $U \rightarrow V$ and U, are *true*. Then on the basis of rule (S 2) in par. 11 the formula V also has to be *true*.

LEMMA 6. Along with the sequent $(K, U)/V$, the sequent $K/U \rightarrow V$ is also valid, and along with the sequent $(K, U \rightarrow V)/U$, the sequent K/U is also valid.

Proof. We only consider the second case and assume that the sequent $(K, U \rightarrow V)/U$ *is* valid, but that the sequent K/U is *not*. We can then choose the truth-values of the atoms $A, B, C, \dots$ in such a way that all formulas in K are *true*, and that the formula U is *false*.

But then the formula $U \rightarrow V$ is *true*, and therefore all formulas in $(K, U \rightarrow V)$ are true, while the formula U is *false*; and that is contrary to the supposition that the sequent $(K, U \rightarrow V)/U$ is valid.

We now prove theorem 4 by observing that the argument in question is constructed from applications of the deduction schemata (i) and (ij^{a-c}). With each step in the argument we can therefore make a corresponding application of lemma 5 or of lemma 6; therefore the sequent K/Z will turn out to be valid.

NOTES

[1] The common objections to the method of proof by contradiction can be found in:
A. Schopenhauer, *Die Welt als Wille und Vorstellung*, 1. Buch, § 15; E. Goblot [1];
R. L. Goodstein [1]; G. Bouligand and J. Desgranges [1]. For the intuitionistic stand-
point one should consult A. Heyting [1]. This method of proof is defended by G. W.
Leibniz, *Nouveaux essais sur l'entendement humain*, IV, viii, § 2; Chr. Sigwart [1];
O. Hölder [1]; G. Polya [1].

About the systematic conversion of an indirect into a direct argumentation one
finds some remarks in L. Löwenheim [1]; comp. R. L. Goodstein, *loc. cit.*; G. Polya,
loc. cit.

* *Annotation*. It is sensible to supplement in the development of a deductive tableau
schema (iij ^{b}) for the negation by a repetition of the formula $\bar{U}$ in the right hand column:

	Premisses	Conclusion
	K	L'
		$\bar{U}$ [$-$ hyp; red. ad abs.]
(iij ^{b})	---	---
	U [$+$ hyp]	$\bar{U}$

Compare schema (iij ^{c}) where the formula U is repeated in the right hand column.
Schema (iij ^{b}) corresponds to the intuitionistically valid form of the *reductio ad absurdum*, schema (iij ^{c}) to the intuitionistically invalid form of this rule of consequence.
Conversions of the deductive tableaux into natural deductions become easier to read
when one always executes these repetitions. Schema (iij ^{b}) can then be read like this: if
one can derive $\bar{U}$ (below the horizontal line) when U is taken as a hypothesis, then U is
to be considered as refuted. The hypothesis can be retracted and $\bar{U}$ (above the line)
asserted. – The application of schema (iij ^{a}) corresponds to an appeal to the rule *ex
falso sequitur quodlibet* in the justification of the lowest (in the tableau) formula of L.

One can say that Beth's method reflects the semantical foundation of these and the
other rules of natural deduction.

** *Annotation*. According to schema (iij ^{c}) formula (1) would have to be repeated in
the right hand column.

*** *Annotation*. Here the manuscript followed with a partial development of a formal
definition of the concepts: a *classical argument* with deduction rule (i), (ij $^{a-c}$).

CHAPTER IV

THE PROBLEM OF LOCKE-BERKELEY

20. AN EXAMPLE

In this chapter I use as a starting point a famous philosophical problem which has been put up for discussion over and over again in the course of the centuries, but which has only been brought completely to a solution in our time.[1] We choose as an example the well-known geometric theorem:

The sum of the angles of a triangle is equal to two right angles.

How the geometrician sets about it if one asks him to prove this theorem has been described in an arresting manner by Kant[2].

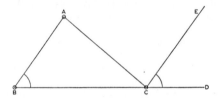

Er fängt sofort davon an, einen Triangel zu konstruieren. Weil er weiss, dass zwei rechte Winkel zusammen gerade soviel austragen, als alle berührenden Winkel, die aus einem Punkte auf einer geraden Linie gezogen werden können, zusammen, so verlängert er eine Seite seines Triangels und bekommt zwei berührende Winkel, die zweien rechten zusammen gleich sind. Nun teilt er den äusseren von diesen Winkeln, indem er eine Linie mit der gegenüberstehenden Seite des Triangels parallel zieht, und sieht, dass hier ein äusserer berührender Winkel entspringe, der einem inneren gleich ist, usw. Er gelangt auf solche Weise durch eine Kette von Schlüssen, immer von der Anschauung geleitet, zur völlig einleuchtenden und zugleich allgemeinen Auflösung der Frage.

21. STATEMENT OF THE PROBLEM AND ATTEMPTS AT ITS SOLUTION

The working method of the geometrician here is indeed characterized in the right manner. Nevertheless a problem urges itself on us here, a problem which at a closer look consists of two questions, i.e.:

(a) Why is it that a proof of a theorem valid for all triangles commonly consists mainly of a consideration which concerns only one particular triangle?

(b) How can one explain that such a consideration nevertheless justifies a universally valid conclusion?

This so-called *problem of Locke-Berkeley* has entertained philosophers, psychologists and pedagogues over and over again; curiously enough logicians have seldom seen a problem here.

One of the first answers to our question has been given by John Locke[3] by means of his *doctrine of abstract ideas*. In his opinion the argumentation of the geometrician does not relate, as one might think, to a concrete triangle but relates to what he calls

the general idea of a triangle, ... for it must be neither oblique nor rectangle, neither equilateral, equicrural, nor scalenon; but all and none of these at once.

This opinion, as we know, has been rejected by Berkeley as patently fallacious, and unquestionably rightly so. Berkeley's own answer[4], though, remains extremely vague; there is little sense in discussing it here. However, I will deal briefly with the solution given by Kant.[5]

Die einzelne hingezeichnete Figur ist empirisch und dient gleichwohl, den Begriff unbeschadet seiner Allgemeinheit, auszudrücken, weil bei dieser empirischen Anschauung immer nur auf die Handlung der Konstruktion des Begriffs, welchem viele Bestimmungen, z.E. der Grösse, der Seiten und der Winkel, ganz gleichgültig sind, gesehen und also von diesen Verschiedenheiten, die den Begriff des Triangels nicht verändern, abstrahiert wird....

Die Mathematik... eilt sogleich zur Anschauung, in welcher sie den Begriff *in concreto* betrachtet, aber doch nicht empirisch, sondern bloss in einer solchen, die sie *a priori* darstellt, d.i. konstruiert hat, und in welcher dasjenige, was aus den allgemeinen Bedingungen der Konstruktion folgt, auch von dem Objekte des konstruierten Begriffs allgemein gelten muss.

With this Kant, strictly speaking, falls back upon the doctrine already defended by Descartes, according to which one reasons in mathematics only seemingly logically but actually reads off a 'Kette von Schlüssen' from a sequence of intuitive insights coupled to a progressive construction. This construction and those insights require, however, an object given in an intuitive vision and by that a particular object.

This point of view, which can also be found in Schopenhauer, has been described by Bolland[6] in the following terms:

Wij mogen stellen, dat reeds in de gewone meetkunde niemand toe komt zonder iets, dan van het standpunt der onvermengde onvervalschte menschelijke logica niets anders dan methodisch geordende onzin, verstandig onverstand kan zijn.

Unquestionably we strike here on one of the roots of the irrationalism of the most recent times.[7] On the other hand we have to mention that a conception closely akin to the view of Descartes and Kant is defended with great consistency in connection with mathematical foundational studies by L. E. J. Brouwer, A. Heyting and their followers. This Amsterdam intuitionism certainly cannot be brought under the heading of rationalism, nor does it fit into the more current forms of contemporary irrationalism.

22. THE EXPOSITION METHOD OF ARISTOTLE

Curiously enough one difficulty completely analogous to the problem of Locke-Berkeley made itself felt already much earlier inside pure logic. Namely in the deduction of the rule for the so-called *conversio simplex* (formulated in the beginning words of the following quotation) Aristotle[8] reasoned in the following way.

If A does not pertain to any B, then likewise B does not pertain to any A. For assume that B pertains to some A, for example c; then it will not be true that A does not pertain to any B; because A pertains to c, which according to assumption is one of the B's.

This reasoning is completely analogous with the geometric argumentation previously considered. It requires that in addition to the universal terms A and B, we introduce an individual object c that then plays the same role as the particular triangle in the reasoning discussed by Kant. In other words here, too, one appeals to *intuitive vision*; this has been brought forward already, notably by Descartes.[9]

It is worth mentioning that the commentator Alexander of Aphrodisias[10] already objected to the so-called *exposition method* applied by Aristotle in this case (and also elsewhere, though sparingly).

The reasoning by exposition [in which an individual object c is 'exposed'] happens in a sensorial manner and not in a syllogistical way; for one takes as exposed object c a sensorially perceptible object c which is a member of A.

This critique on Aristotle has been accepted by tradition. This is expressed in a striking way in a statement of P. Richard (cited by J. Maritain[11]) who moreover connects both cases discussed here; this connection is remarked but rarely.

La forme syllogistique joue dans ce cas le même rôle que l'objet matériel ou la figure tracée sur le tableau qui aide à certaines démonstrations.

For that matter, Aristotle himself also already alludes now and then to problems which at least are strongly analogous to the problem of Locke-Berkeley.[12]

One has for that reason also contended that it is necessary to assume something that is false just as it also happens that the geometricians consider something as being one foot long although its length does not equal one foot at all. But something like that cannot occur at all. For the geometricians don't assume something that is false (as in the formal argumentation such a premiss does not play any role)....

Should we accept with Descartes, Kant, Bolland and Brouwer (to mention just a few) the point of view, according to which in mathematical argumentations a non-logical element is indispensible (even stronger; according to which mathematical argumentation only seemingly has a logical character, while in reality the reasoning proceeds by way of intuitive constructions), then we would have to admit equally, on the grounds of the remark made by Alexander, that this non-logical element plays a role, too, in the construction of the theory of syllogism. This was apparently denied by Aristotle himself.

23. APPEAL TO THE METHOD OF SEMANTIC TABLEAUX

In relation to the latter case, however, we can easily see that Aristotle is in the right.

The premiss: *A does not pertain to any B*, and the conclusion: *B does not pertain to any A*, we represent respectively by the formulas:

$$(1) \quad (x)\,[B(x) \to \overline{A(x)}],$$
$$(2) \quad (y)\,[A(y) \to \overline{B(y)}].$$

We will show that the conclusion (2) *follows logically* from the premiss (1); i.e., that it can't occur that the premiss (1) is *true* and that simultaneously the conclusion (2) is *false*. For that purpose we construct a semantic tableau.

True		False	
(1) $(x)[B(x)\to\overline{A(x)}]$		(2) $(y)[A(y)\to\overline{B(y)}]$	
		(3) $A(c)\to B(c)$	
(4) $A(c)$		(5) $\overline{B(c)}$	
(6) $B(c)$			
(7) $B(c)\to\overline{A(c)}$			

1	2	1	2
	(9) $\overline{A(c)}$	(8) $B(c)$	(10) $A(c)$

As the tableau closes it becomes apparent that the conclusion (2) indeed follows logically from the premiss (1).* By conversion of the tableau we obtain the following argument.

$$
\begin{array}{lll}
(1) & (x)[B(x)\to\overline{A(x)}] & [\text{prem}] \\
& \cdots\cdots\cdots\cdots\cdots & \\
(4) & A(c) & [+\text{hyp } 1] \\
& \text{----------} & \\
(6) & B(c) & [+\text{hyp } 2] \\
(7) & B(c)\to\overline{A(c)} & (1) \\
(8) & B(c) & (6) \\
(9) & \overline{A(c)} & (7), (8) \\
(10) & A(c) & (4) \\
& \text{----------} & \\
(5) & \overline{B(c)} & [-\text{hyp } 2] \\
& \cdots\cdots\cdots\cdots\cdots & \\
(3) & A(c)\to\overline{B(c)} & [-\text{hyp } 1] \\
(2) & (y)[A(y)\to\overline{B(y)}] & (3)
\end{array}
$$

Not only does this argument reflect the deduction given by Aristotle for the rule for *conversio simplex*, it also furnishes striking support for his rejection of the conception that geometricians at times would appeal to false premisses. In our reasoning we indeed appeal to the formulas (4) $A(c)$ and (6) $B(c)$ which cannot both be true, as can be seen from the conclusion. These formulas, however, do not occur as premisses but only as hypotheses which are introduced at a certain point and eliminated afterwards.

In an analogous way we can now also analyze the argumentation described by Kant. The condition that X, Y, Z determine a triangle is expressed by $Tr(X, Y, Z)$; the condition that the sum of the angles in this triangle is equal to two right angles will be expressed by a more complicated formula, which we abbreviate to $U(X, Y, Z)$. The geometric axioms (joined together in one formula) appear as premisses; the theorem to be proved as conclusion:

$$(2) \quad (X)(Y)(Z)[Tr(X, Y, Z) \rightarrow U(X, Y, Z)].$$

Our tableau therefore takes the following form;

True	False
(1) Geometric axioms	(2) $(X)(Y)(Z)[Tr(X, Y, Z) \rightarrow U(X, Y, Z)]$
	(3) $(Y)(Z)[Tr(A, Y, Z) \rightarrow U(A, Y, Z)]$
	(4) $(Z)[Tr(A, B, Z) \rightarrow U(A, B, Z)]$
	(5) $Tr(A, B, C) \rightarrow U(A, B, C)$
(6) $Tr(A, B, C)$	(7) $U(A, B, C)$
.	.
.	.
.	.

As the conclusion (7) follows logically from the premisses, in the long run this semantic tableau, too, has to close.

By conversion of the closed tableau we again obtain a classical deduction, for which we can foresee the structure in rough lines.

(1)   Geometric axioms   [prem]
----
(6) $Tr(A, B, C)$ [+ hyp 1]
          .
          .
          .
(7) $U(A, B, C)$
----
(5) $Tr(A, B, C) \rightarrow U(A, B, C)$ [− hyp 1]

(4) $(Z) [Tr (A, B, Z) \rightarrow U (A, B, Z)]$
(3) $(Y) (Z) [Tr (A, Y, Z) \rightarrow U (A, Y, Z)]$
(2) $(X) (Y) (Z) [Tr (X, Y, Z) \rightarrow U (X, Y, Z)]$

This structure completely satisfies the description given by Kant. The argumentation begins with the introduction of three special points, A, B, and C, of which it is assumed that they form a triangle. To this figure the general geometric axioms are applied, after which one continues the argument until conclusion (7) appears. Then hypothesis (6) is eliminated so that conclusion (5) is no longer encumbered with the original supposition about the points A, B, C. On this basis generalizations are possible, by which conclusion (2) is finally obtained.

We are now able to respond to the problem of Locke-Berkeley as follows. Regarding question (a): the introduction of the special points A, B, C, is motivated by the manner in which a formula as conclusion (2) is to be treated in the construction of the semantic tableau. With that, though, question (b) has also been answered: if the semantic tableau closes, then it is determined that the conclusion follows logically from the premises.

An appeal to the hypotheses which have been introduced need not cause undue concern provided that these hypotheses are eliminated in due time in the correct way.

A comparison with the first example strengthens our opinion that the structure of the obtained deduction is not related to the necessity of an appeal to intuitive vision, and that there is no essential difference between a formal-logical and a geometric process of reasoning. The structure of both reasonings is determined by the form of the premises and conclusion in connection with the meaning pertaining to the logical symbols.

24. THE COMPLETENESS PROBLEM – INFORMAL AND HEURISTIC DEDUCTION METHODS

One could put forward the following objection to the solution proposed here to the problem of Locke-Berkeley. The fact that some argumentations, which seem at first sight to involve an appeal to intuitive vision, nevertheless can be converted into a purely formal logical deduction, does not prove that such a conversion is in other cases also always possible. It remains possible to think that some sound reasonings require an appeal to certain intuitive insights.

To invalidate this objection we will have to make use of all the logical insights acquired up to now and to supplement and deepen these at certain points. In this connection may I first point to the following observations.

1. A reasoning that proceeds from the premiss K and yields the conclusion Z is sound if and only if it admits no counter-example (par. 2).

2. The construction of a semantic tableau for the sequent K/Z is a systematic attempt to construct such a counterexample (par. 5).

3. If the semantic tableau for the sequent K/Z closes, then there is no suitable counterexample; Z is in that case a logical consequence of K.

4. By the conversion of the closed semantic tableau for the sequent K/Z, one can obtain a deduction of Z from K (par. 6); this deduction admits no counterexample and therefore is sound.

Suppose now that Z can be obtained on the grounds of K, but only by an appeal to intuitive vision. The semantic tableau for the sequent K/Z cannot then be closed, as otherwise according to 4. a formal-logical deduction of Z from K would be possible. On the other hand, even though it is not closed, the tableau in question cannot possibly yield a suitable counterexample, as otherwise the deduction of Z from K would not be sound. Briefly said;

5. If a sound deduction of Z from K is possible, but only on account of an appeal to intuitive (or other non-logical) considerations, then the semantic tableau for the sequent K/Z cannot be closed, but neither can it yield a suitable counterexample.

One can, however, also prove:

6. A non-closed semantic tableau for the sequent K/Z always yields a suitable counterexample in proof of the fact that a sound deduction of Z from K is not possible.

From 5. and 6. again follows:

7. If a sound deduction of Z from K is possible, then a formal-logical deduction of Z from K is also always possible.

This theorem, which has been proved with respect to elementary predicate logic in 1930 by K. Gödel, is known as the *completeness theorem* for this logical system.

For purely implicational logic we have proved in par. 19 a completely analogous theorem, with the understanding that we considered a suitable collection of truth values instead of a suitable counterexample as in this case. Nevertheless in broad outline we use the same argument as in par. 19.

We take into account formulas which can contain the implication sign $\rightarrow$, the negation sign $-$ and the universal quantifiers (x), (y), (z),.... In the construction of a semantic tableau we will therefore have to have at our disposal the closure schema (i), the reduction schemata (ij^a) and (ij^b) for implication and the reduction schemata (iij^a) and (iij^b) for negation. To obviate the difficulties resulting from the possible "supplanting" of formulas we can at will avail ourselves of the improper reduction schemata (ij^c) and (iij^c). Finally, we obtain for the universal quantifiers the reduction schemata:

	True	False		True	False
	K'	L		K	L'
	$(v)\,U\,(v)$				$(v)\,U\,(v)$
(iv^a)	$\overline{}$		(iv^b)		$\overline{}$
	$U\,(p)$				$U\,(p)$

In (iv^a) the parameter p can be freely chosen; in (iv^b) a parameter p must be chosen that does not yet occur in the tableau.

To the deduction schemata already described in par. 19 we can now add the following.

(iij^a)	(iij^b)	(iij^c)	(iv^a)	(iv^b)
K'	K	K	K'	K
$U, \bar{U}$	U	$\bar{U}$	$(v)\,U\,(v)$	$[U\,(p)]$
$\overline{V}$	$\overline{\bar{U}}$	$\overline{U}$	$\overline{U\,(p)}$	$\overline{(v)\,U\,(v)}$
	$\cdots\cdots$	$\cdots\cdots$		
	$\bar{U}$	U		

In deduction schema (iv^b) the parameter p may not appear in K or in $(v)\,U\,(v)$. As an illustration of these things I refer to the tableau and the deduction on p. 46. In the tableau, formula 7 arises from formula 1 by application of the reduction schema (iv^a), and formula (3) from formula (2) by application of the reduction schema (iv^b). In accordance with that, formula (7) arises in the deduction by application of the deduction schema (iv^a) to formula (1) and formula (2) by application of the deduction schema (iv^b) to formula (3). This application of deduction schema (iv^b) is justifiable as formula (3) only depends on formula (1) which does not contain the parameter c.

THEOREM 7. Theorem 1 correspondingly applies to the version considered here of elementary predicate logic.

We will reduce this theorem again to two lemmas, but by way of introduction we first consider a variant on the example given in par. 7 *sub* (3).

	True				False	
(1)	$(x)\,(y)\,\overline{A(x,y)}$			(2)	$(z)\,\overline{(t)\,A(t,z)}$	
(3)	$(z)\,(t)\,A(t,z)$	(2)		(6)	$(y)\,\overline{A(a,y)}$	(4)
(4)	$(y)\,\overline{A(a,y)}$	(1)		(7)	$\overline{(t)\,A(t,a)}$	(5)
(5)	$(t)\,A(t,a)$	(3)		(8)	$A(a,b)$	(6)
(10)	$A(a,b)$	(8)		9)	$A(c,a)$	(7)
(11)	$(y)\,\overline{A(b,y)}$	(1)		(15)	$(y)\,\overline{A(b,y)}$	(11)
(12)	$(y)\,\overline{A(c,y)}$	(1)		(16)	$(y)\,\overline{A(c,y)}$	(12)
(13)	$(t)\,A(t,b)$	(3)		(17)	$(t)\,A(t,b)$	(13)
(14)	$(t)\,A(t,c)$	(3)		(18)	$(t)\,A(t,c)$	(14)
(23)	$A(b,d)$	(19)		(19)	$A(b,d)$	(15)
(24)	$A(c,e)$	(20)		(20)	$A(c,e)$	(16)
	$\cdot$			(21)	$A(f,b)$	(17)
	$\cdot$			(22)	$A(g,c)$	(18)
	$\cdot$				$\cdot$	
					$\cdot$	
					$\cdot$	

It is clear that the tableau does not close and that its construction leads to a *regressus in infinitum*. Nevertheless we have to try to read off from the tableau a suitable counterexample to the sequent:

$$(x)\,(y)\,\overline{A(x,y)}/(z)\,\overline{(t)\,A(t,z)}$$

In doing this we must bear in mind what has been said about the *interpretation* of formulas in par. 5 *sub* (4).

We consider the parameters $a, b, c, \ldots$ as names of individual objects which we will denote in this discussion as **a, b, c,** …; the term A expresses a binary predicate **A**, which we will presently describe more clearly. Further we made an appeal in the interpretation to a non-empty domain **D**, which we will establish presently. This domain **D** has to contain all objects **a, b, c,** … as elements. Evidently we identify **D** with the set of just these objects.

We now have to describe the binary predicate **A** in such a manner that its application is determined for the elements of the domain **D**. So let **p** and **q** be elements of **D**. These elements have got names p and q. We now say that the predicate **A** applies to **p** in relation to **q**, if and only if the formula $A(p, q)$ occurs in the left hand column of our tableau.

The interpretation of the formulas is now completely determined. By this interpretation *all* formulas in the left hand column of our tableau are *true* and *all* formulas in the right hand column are *false*.

1. For the atoms $A(p, q)$ this is almost self-evident. We first consider the formula $A(a, b)$. This formula occurs in the left hand column. According to the description of the predicate **A**, this predicate then applies to **a** in relation to **b**. On the other hand $A(a, b)$ expresses the condition that the predicate **A** applies to **a** in relation to **b**. Because this application is correct, the formula $A(a, b)$ is *true*.

The formula $A(c, a)$ occurs in the right hand column. So this formula cannot occur in the left hand column, as this would have brought the tableau to closure. So the predicate **A** does *not* apply to **c** in relation to **a**. The formula $A(a, c)$, which expresses the condition that the predicate **A** applies to **c** in relation to **a**, is therefore false. –

For the sequel it is helpful to designate a formula U as *rightly placed* if it occurs in the left hand column and is *true*, or if it occurs in the right hand column and is *false*. So we can briefly formulate the conclusion of the discussion under 1 by saying that an atom $A(p, q)$ is always rightly placed.

2. If U is rightly placed then $\bar{U}$ cannot be wrongly placed. For assume that $\bar{U}$ is wrongly placed. Then there are two possibilities.

a. $\bar{U}$ occurs in the left hand column but is false. In that case U must be true. In addition the presence of $\bar{U}$ in the left hand column gives rise to an application of the reduction schema (iij^a) by which U appears in the right hand column. But then U is wrongly placed, contrary to assumption.

b. $\bar{U}$ occurs in the right hand column but is true. We can exclude this possibility in an analogous manner.

3. If all formulas $U(a)$, $U(b)$, $U(c)$, ... are rightly placed, then $(x) U(x)$ cannot be wrongly placed. For assume that $(x) U(x)$ is wrongly placed. There are again two possibilities.

a. $(x) U(x)$ occurs in the left hand column but is false. Then some formula $U(p)$ has to be false. The presence of $(x) U(x)$ in the left hand column gives rise to a sequence of applications of the reduction schema (iv^a) by which consecutively all formulas $U(a)$, $U(b)$, $U(c)$, ... appear in the left hand column.** Then, however, $U(p)$ is wrongly placed contrary to assumption.

b. $(x) U(x)$ occurs in the right hand column but is true. This case is again treated in an analogous manner. –
In the case of our example with this we are done. Formula (2) is rightly placed, because formula (3) is rightly placed; formula (3) is rightly placed because formulas (5), (13), (14), ... are rightly placed. The last-named formulas are rightly placed because formulas (7), (17), (18), ... are rightly placed. And these formulas are rightly placed because all atoms are rightly placed.

For the sake of the general purport of this discussion we will also consider the remaining case.

4. If U and V are rightly placed, $U \rightarrow V$ is also rightly placed. For assume that $U \rightarrow V$ is wrongly placed. Then there are again two possibilities of which we discuss only one. Assume that $U \rightarrow V$ occurs in the right hand column but is true. The presence of $U \rightarrow V$ leads to an application of reduction schema (ij^b) by which U appears left and V right. Because U and V are rightly placed, U is true and V is false; but then according to the rule (S 2) the formula $U \rightarrow V$ is false, contrary to supposition. –

It will benefit the clarity of my argument, if at this point I introduce and explain a number of current technical terms, some of which I have used already incidentally.

When the formulas in a sequent K/L, or:

$$(U_1, U_2, ..., U_m)/(V_1, V_2, ..., V_n),$$

do not contain merely one binary predicate parameter A, but say two binary predicate parameters A and B and in addition two unary predicate parameters S and T, then a counterexample will involve, besides the domain **D** of individual objects (often denoted as the '*universe of discourse*'), two binary predicates **A** and **B** and two unary predicates **S** and **T**. An arbitrarily chosen combination $\langle$**D, A, B, S, T**$\rangle$ is denoted as a *structure*.[13] We will denote arbitrary structures by **M**, **M′, M″**,..., **N, N′**,....

If a formula U is *true* with regard to a given structure **M**, then we also say that the structure **M** is a *model* for the formula U. A *counterexample* in relation to a sequent K/L is a structure **M** which is a model for all formulas U in K without being a model for any of the formulas V in L. A sequent K/L which admits no counterexample is denoted as *valid*.

If the sequent K/Z is valid, then every model **M** for (all formulas U in) K is at the same time a model for Z; we also say that Z *follows logically* from K. If Z follows logically from the empty set $\emptyset$, then we call Z a *logical identity*; a logical identity is *true* with regard to any structure **M**.

A semantic tableau for a sequent K/L can be conceived as a description of a *systematic* attempt to construct a counterexample in relation to this sequent. Once again I draw attention to the *two* aspects of the systematic character of the construction. If the semantic tableau closes, then it follows from that that no counterexample can exist; so the sequent K/L is valid.

If the semantic tableau does not close, then it yields a counterexample as desired. This is at least the intent, and in the case we considered as an example we could indeed read off from the tableau a suitable counterexample $\langle$**D, A**$\rangle$. Now it is true that this example was too simple to enable us to hold it as a paradigma, but it is still worth the trouble to unravel the fabric of the good result reached in this case.

a. The predicate **A** was chosen in such a way that all atoms $A(p, q)$ got the desired truth value.

b. The formulas $\bar{U}$ and $U \rightarrow V$ got the right truth value because the semantical rules (S 2) and (S 3) are *reversible*. Suppose for example that the formula $U \rightarrow V$ occurs in the right hand column. We then apply reduction schema (ij^b), in other words we say: for $U \to V$ to be false U has to be true and V false. In reading off the counterexample we say conversely: if U is *true* and V is *false*, then $U \to V$ is *false*.

c. By the choice of **D** we have insured that the formulas $(x) \, U \, (x)$ received the required truth values. Suppose first that $(x) \, U \, (x)$ occurs in the left hand column. The application of reduction schema (iv^a) then leads to the appearance of all formulas $U \, (a)$, $U \, (b)$, $U \, (c)$,... in the left hand column. In reading off the counterexample we say: the formulas $U \, (a)$, $U \, (b)$, $U \, (c)$,... are all true and the domain **D** does not contain objects other than **a**, **b**, **c**,...; thus the formula $(x) \, U \, (x)$ is true.

Now suppose that $(x) \, U \, (x)$ occurs in the right hand column. The application of reduction schema (iv^b) now makes a certain formula $U \, (p)$ appear in the right hand column. In reading off the counterexample we say: the formula $U \, (p)$ is false and the domain **D** contains the object **p**: thus the formula $(x) \, U \, (x)$ is false.

Our example cannot without further ado be held as a paradigma, because the complications that can result from possible splittings in sub-tableaux did not occur in this particular case. If in the left hand column a formula:

$$(x) \, [U \, (x) \to V \, (x)]$$

occurs, then consecutively all formulas

$$U \, (a) \to V \, (a), \; U \, (b) \to V \, (b), \; U \, (c) \to V \, (c), \ldots$$

can appear in this column, and each of these formulas gives rise to a splitting of each subtableau.

Of the subtableaux which originate in this manner many may, of course, eventually close. But if the tableau as a whole does not close, then it must be possible to detach from the tableau a connected sequence of sub-tableaux which fit into each other, in which no splittings

The existence of such a sequence of subtableaux can be demonstrated in the following way. The internal structure of a semantic tableau can be characterized in a striking way by means of a *tree*.

In the construction of the tree, which corresponds to a given semantic tableau, we neglect the distinction between the left and the right hand column. Each formula in the tableau is represented by a point of the tree, and each splitting of the tableau is indicated by a branching of the tree.

The tree B in the above figure corresponds to the second semantic tableau in par. 5. We shall now prove:

If a tree B contains an infinite number of points, then it possesses a branch which runs on indefinitely.

To each point P on B corresponds a configuration $B^{(P)}$ which consists of all points Q on B which lie on a branch which also contains P. In the above figure the configurations $B^{(11)}$ and $B^{(12)}$ have been reproduced for the case of our example. Of course always $B^{(1)} = B$. It is easy to see that $B^{(P)}$ is again a tree.

We now say that P on B is a *point of the first kind* if $B^{(P)}$ contains only a finite number of points; if $B^{(P)}$ contains an infinite number of points then P is a *point of the second kind* on B. The points of the second kind on B form a configuration B^+. It is easy to see that B^+ is again a tree and that a point P on B^+ can never be an end point. If the number of points on B is finite, then B^+ does not contain a single point.

We now suppose however that $B = B^{(1)}$ contains infinitely many points. So the point 1 is of the second kind on B, and therefore lies on B^+. As B^+ does not contain any end point, in point 1 there must start at least one branch of B^+ that runs on indefinitely. This branch must belong to B at the same time, thus substantiating our proof.

We deal now with the detached segment of the tableau in the manner we described in our example. Everything which was said is still applicable and so we find a counterexample **M** with regard to the considered sequent K/L. We will just investigate the truth value of the formula:

$$(x) [U(x) \to V(x)]$$

in the left hand column. This formula also occurs in the left hand column of the detached segment of the tableau and so we also find all the formulas

$$U(a) \to V(a), \ U(b) \to V(b), \ U(c) \to V(c), \ldots$$

there. Each of these formulas requires an application of reduction schema (ij^a) and therefore gives rise to a splitting.

Of the two subtableaux that originate in this way, one will in every case turn up in the detached segment. We will find there $U(a)$ right or $V(a)$ left, $U(b)$ right or $V(b)$ left, $U(c)$ right or $V(c)$ left, …. Assuming that these formulas, in so far as they occur in the detached segment are rightly placed there, we can then conclude that $U(a)$ will be false or $V(a)$ true,

$U(b)$ will be false or $V(b)$ true, $U(c)$ will be false or $V(c)$ true, …. But then all formulas $U(a) \to V(a)$, $U(b) \to V(b)$, $U(c) \to V(c)$, … will be true and so will the formula:

$$(x)\,[(U(x) \to V(x)]$$

This formula is therefore also rightly placed.

LEMMA 8. If the sequent K/L is valid, then the semantic tableau for that sequent closes.

Proof. Assume that the tableau does not close. It then yields in the manner just described a counterexample **M** with regard to the sequent K/L. But this sequent is valid, and therefore does not admit a counterexample. So the semantic tableau has to be closed.

LEMMA 9. If the semantic tableau for the sequent K/Z is closed, then there is a classical argument as described in theorem 1.

Proof. We can apply the proof of lemma 3 without change.

Theorem 7 is now an immediate consequence of the lemma's 8 and 9. For theorem 7 the following inverse again holds;

THEOREM 10. Theorem 4 correspondingly applies to the version of elementary predicate logic considered here.

This theorem again can be reduced to some lemma's.

LEMMA 11. The sequents $(K', U, \bar{U})/V$ and $(K', (v)\,U(v))/U(p)$ are valid.

LEMMA 12. With the sequent $(K, U)/\bar{U}$ also the sequent $K/\bar{U}$ is valid; and with the sequent $(K, \bar{U})/U$ also the sequent K/U is valid.

LEMMA 13. If the parameter p does not occur in either K or $(v)\,U(v)$, then with the sequent $K/U(p)$ also the sequent $K/(v)\,U(v)$ is valid.

The proof of these lemmas does not present any difficulties, and from the lemmas 5, 6 (p. 42) and 11–13 theorem 10 follows immediately. –

Thus far we did not take into account formulas which contain the disjunction sign $\vee$, the conjunction sign &, the double implication sign $\leftrightarrow$ or the existential quantifiers (Ex), (Ey), (Ez), …. This implies no essential restriction, though, because we can consider

$U \vee V$ as an abbreviation for $U \rightarrow V$,

$U \& V$ „ „   „   „ $\overline{U \rightarrow \overline{V}}$

$U \leftrightarrow V$ „ „   „   „ $(U \rightarrow V) \& (V \rightarrow U)$,

$(Ev)\, U\,(v)$ „ „   „   „ $(v)\, \overline{U\,(v)}$

We thus obtain immediately:

THEOREM 14. Theorems 1 and 4 correspondingly apply to the usual restricted version of elementary logic.

Theorem 14, which forms a résumé of the theorems 1, 4, 7, and 10, brings out the good properties of the deduction method for elementary logic developed in the above. This method is *reliable* (comp. theorem 4): the correct application of it can never yield a reasoning which could be invalidated by counterexamples. It is at the same time also *complete* (comp. theorem 1): if a sound deduction of Z from K is possible, then the method developed here will yield such a deduction.

Our deduction method, however, also has *les défauts de ses qualités* which, for that matter, it has in common with all equivalent methods: its correct application is cumbersome and time consuming. One should not be misled by the simplicity of the examples given: the considered deductions are best characterized as detailed analysis of steps of proof of which one usually in 'real' argumentations takes a few at the same time.

The application of our deduction method leads in practice to *two* difficulties, which for the sake of a good insight should be well-distinguished. In the first instance it is often difficult to find the correct deduction of a conclusion Z from a class of premisses K; in the second it is sometimes difficult to formulate a deduction clearly once it is found.

The second difficulty one avoids in practice, usually by merely formulating the main points of the deduction and leaving a number of matters of secondary importance unmentioned. In the mean time one should distinguish in this connection two possible cases. Who applies the modus CELANTES (par. 3) reasons as follows:

$$\overline{(Ex)\,[M\,(x)\,\&\,P\,(x)]}$$
$$(y)\,[S\,(y) \rightarrow M\,(y)]$$
$$\therefore \overline{(Ez)\,[P\,(z)\,\&\,S\,(z)]}$$

and thus leaves out of a correct argument (par. 6) *eight* steps. Now he can do this in the first instance with an express reference to a complete deduction as given in par. 6. In this case he uses the modus CELANTES as a *derived deduction schema*. It is clear that, by making a certain supply of derived deduction schemata, one can in this manner formulate argumentations in a very concise manner without detracting from formal rigor.

In the second place one can avail oneself of a more concise manner of reasoning without expressly justifying or even mentioning this. In this case one avails oneself an *informal method of deduction*. In current practice of science one almost always goes to work in this manner. Thus one trusts insight and practice and leaves the further analysis of the informal argumentations to specialists in the area of logic and foundational studies.

The first difficulty, which concerned the *finding* of correct deductions, has not been met in any way by this, however. The finding of a convincing informal proof is generally more difficult than the analysis which enables a conversion of the informal proof into a formal deduction; if the analysis presents particular difficulties, then this often means that one has been wrongly convinced by the informal proof.

The completeness theorem guarantees us that, *if* Z follows logically from K, there also has to be a correct deduction of Z from K. *That* Z follows logically from K, however, (apart from exceptional cases which do not matter here), as long as this deduction has not been given, we can only *presume*.

Heuristic methods of deduction are generally intended to give us indications about what has to be done, if such a presumption arises. An heuristic method of deduction cannot be equivalent to the formal method of deduction developed above, as its application would otherwise present the same difficulties; an heuristic method of deduction, therefore, will have to abandon either reliability or completeness. In practice this means that reliability is sacrificed; that is not as bad as it looks, because an heuristic method makes no pretense of yielding definitive results.

It is in the nature of the matter that about heuristics *in abstracto* one cannot say very much that makes sense; I will therefore restrict myself to indicating some points of view.

1. If there is a suspicion present that the conclusion Z is derivable from the set of premisses K, but the execution of the deduction presents un-

foreseen difficulties, it would be good for one to realize the grounds on which the presumption is based. It can for example be that the sought after conclusion Z forms a résumé or rounding off of a certain number of conclusions $Z_1, Z_2, \ldots$ which one already has been able to deduce from the premisses in K, or that Z forms an analogon of certain conclusion $Z_1, Z_2, \ldots$ which one has obtained from sets of premisses $K_1, K_2, \ldots$ which are analogous to K. In such cases it is useful to look for common characteristics in the already available deductions of $Z_1, Z_2, \ldots$. By combining fragments of all these deductions one will then perhaps obtain a rough draft for a deduction of Z from K.

2. In the event that the investigation described above yields no satisfactory result, for example if in the obtained draft there remain demonstrable gaps which are difficult to fill, then slowly there appear grounds for the suspicion that Z is *not* derivable from K. We will then try to elucidate this suspicion by aid of the means of construction of a counterexample; for this construction we shall find directives if we pay attention to the gaps in the draft construction.

3. One often points to the usefulness of empirical considerations for heuristics. However, it appears to me that we have already got to know the most prominent forms of application of such considerations under 1 and 2.

4. One often points out, and very rightly so, that in drawing up a deduction from Z to K, one has to direct oneself to the *form* of (premisses and) conclusion. If Z has the form of negation Y, then we try to carry Y *ad absurdum*; if Z has the form of a general proposition $(x) U (x)$ then we try to prove $U (p)$ for arbitrary p; and so on. This direction is completely to the point, but by introducing the method of semantic tableaux we have already taken it into account *a priori*.

5. Finally one usually points out that there exist for certain areas of science specific methods of deduction. So one has at his disposal in the theory of natural numbers the *method of recurrence* or *of complete induction*:

$$U\,(O)$$
$$\frac{(n)\,[\,U\,(n) \to U\,(n+1)]}{}$$
$$(n)\,U\,(n),$$

with its different variants.

NOTES

[1] For further historical data, comp. E. W. Beth [94].
[2] I. Kant, *Kritik der reinen Vernunft*, A 716.
[3] J. Locke, *An Essay Concerning Human Understanding*, Book IV, Ch. 7, § 9.
[4] G. Berkeley, *A Treatise Concerning the Principles of Human Knowledge*, Introduction, §§ 12–16.
[5] I. Kant, *Kritik der reinen Vernunft*, A 713ff.
[6] G. J. P. J. Bolland [1].
[7] Comp. E. W. Beth [S].
[8] Aristoteles, *Analytica priora* A 2, 25ᵃ 15.
[9] Verg. E. W. Beth [102].
[10] *Alexandri in Aristotelis Analyticorum Priorum Librum I Commentarium*, ed. M. Wallies, Berolini 1883, p. 32.
[11] J. Maritain [1] p. 278.
[12] Aristoteles, *Metaphysica* N 2, 1089ᵃ 21–25.
[13] To avoid needless difficulties, I will just point out that in the literature on modern logic the terms 'structure' and 'model' are also used in other connections and in a different meaning than here; this should not be ascribed to philosophical or other differences of opinion.

* *Annotation.* For formula (2) to be false in the present tableau, **D** will have to contain at least one individual which, as value of y, does not satisfy the condition $A(y) \to \overline{B\,(y)}$; if we denote this individual by c, then formula (3) will have to be false. Compare what was said under (6) on p. 17 and schema (ivᵇ) on p. 53.
** *Annotation.* The application of reduction schema (ivᵃ) will have to be understood here and in the sequel as obligatory (and not merely admissable) for each individual parameter p which is enjoined in the interpretation to an individual **p** of the domain **D**.

CHAPTER V

ON THE SO-CALLED 'THOUGHT MACHINE'

25. INTRODUCTION

Modern computers do not only perform much faster tasks which are already feasible for older calculating machines, but are also fit for more refined, more complicated and more differentiated operations. In particular operations such as self-correction and self-programming make one think almost irresistably of 'intelligent' and 'human' behavior. For that reason it is no wonder that one has begun to speak of '*thinking machines*'. There is no longer a large step needed to arrive at the notion of a '*thought machine*', even if that is something completely different.

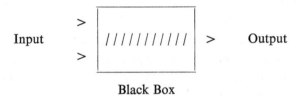

Black Box

There is, for that matter, still another circumstance which can lead one's thoughts in this direction. Namely, one sometimes speaks of 'logical calculating automata'. Here one alludes to the fact that these automata are based on binary arithmetic. This binary arithmetic has in its turn connections with classical (two-valued) sentential logic. On the other hand, *logic* also has something to do with *thinking*.

26. BINARY ARITHMETIC AND LOGIC

The connection between binary arithmetic and classical sentential logic may be explained briefly with the aid of a table (see next page). In binary arithmetic base *two* assumes the role played by base *ten* in 'normal' decimal arithmetic. Natural numbers are therefore written with the figures 0 and 1, whereby the figure which expresses the units, comes

x	y	$x+y$	$x.y$	$x \& y$	$(x \& \bar{y}) \quad \vee \quad (\bar{x} \& y)$
0	0	00	0	0	0
0	1	01	0	0	1
1	0	01	0	0	1
1	1	10	1	1	0

completely on the right. Then the next left figure will represent the two's, and so on. If so desired we can add other figures 0 on the left, because these do not contribute to the numerical value. Therefore for the numbers from *zero* through *fifteen* the following notation is used:

0,	1,	10,	11,	100,	101,	110,	111,
1000,	1001,	1010,	1011,	1100,	1101,	1110,	1111,

or, with the addition of figures 0:

0000,	0001,	0010,	0011,	0100,	0101,	0110,	0111,
1000,	1001,	1010,	1011,	1100,	1101,	1110,	1111.

In the tables of addition and multiplication we only have to mention the values of $x+y$ and of $x.y$ for $x=0$ and $y=0$, $x=0$ and $y=1$, $x=1$ and $y=0$, $x=1$ and $y=1$, in binary notation. One will find these values in the thrid and fourth column of the table.

Futhermore in logic we can replace the truth values *true* and *false* by numerical values 1 and 0. Instead of: 'U is *true*' we then say '$w(U)=1$'. The semantic rule (S 2) in par. 11 can then be formulated as follows:

(S 2) $w(U \rightarrow V)=1$, if $w(U)=0$ or $w(V)=1$; $w(U \rightarrow V)=0$, if $w(U)=1$ and $w(V)=0$.

In the fifth and sixth column of the table certain truth values of $x \& y$ and

$$(x \& \bar{y}) \vee (\bar{x} \& y)$$

are also mentioned. The figures in the fifth column concur with the figures in the two's place in the third column and also with the figures in the fourth column; and the figures in the sixth column concur with the figures in the unit's place in the third column.

We can moreover describe certain properties of electrical switching circuits in a simple manner with the aid of logical formulas. Let 0 stand for 'conducting no current', and 1 stand for 'conducting a current'. An element obtained by parallel connection of the elements x and y can then be denoted by $x \vee y$; by connection x and y in series we obtain $x \& y$. If the element x is connected with a second element by means of a relay in such a way that a flow of current through x cuts off the current through the second element, then this second element can be denoted by $\bar{x}$.

If we now replace first the operations of binary arithmetic by logical operations, and if we subsequently realize these logical operations by means of suitable electrical connections, then we obtain a switching circuit suitable for calculations.

27. SPECIFIC OPERATIONS OF THE HUMAN INTELLECT

The speculations briefly indicated in par. 1 have brought some authors to question the extent in which one has the right to speak of human intelligence with respect to computers. According to others, though, even asking such questions has no meaning.

In my opinion one *can* give meaning to questions such as those meant here, on the condition, however, that one agrees beforehand as to which operations have to be considered characteristic for the human intellect. I intend to deal with this question in full presently.

I will first attempt to give a closer description of the operations which should be deemed characteristic of a computer. As such I would like to name in this connection: *acquisition*, *assimilation* and *conversion* of information. Communication, as *transport* of information, I shall have to leave out of my argument. I also forego a closer analysis of the concept of *information*.

One usually designates the specific operations of the human intellect altogether as '*thinking*'. Thinking however can take very divergent forms, of which I would like to name the following here:
  (1) Meditation,
  (2) Induction,
  (3) Deliberation as preparation to the taking of a decision of the will,
  (4) Deliberation as preparation to the execution of a practical act,
  (5) Reasoning as argumentative thinking,
  (6) Appraising or adjudging.

In connection with our subject we have to think more specifically of the following operations, in which the intellect takes a predominant share:

(1) Translating,

(2) Abstracting,

(3) The solution of mathematical problems, and notably mathematical argumentation,

(4) Playing chess.

I will here particularly go into thinking as *mathematical argumentation* as this has been at all times recognized as a pre-eminently characteristic manifestation of the human intellect. As a special aspect of the question to what extent one has the right to speak with regard to computers of human intelligence, I therefore consider here the question of the possibility of *'simulating'* reasoning or argumentative thinking as this expresses itself, notably in mathematics, with the aid of suitable computers (better: with the aid of suitable programming of computers).

With this, at the same time, the concept of a 'thought machine' has been given a somewhat closer description. This description, as all descriptions, contains a certain restriction because the possibility of simulating translating, abstracting or playing chess will further have to stay out of consideration. On the other hand, though, a deeper insight as to the possibility of the automatization of reasoning will undoubtably contribute, as well, to the clarification with regard to these problems which I will have to leave out of consideration here. For the problems concerning translating, abstracting and chess playing this will surely be beyond dispute.

Many persons will, however, want a separate discussion for example of the question about the possibility of the automatization of appraising or adjudging. My answer to this question will be brief and perhaps paradoxical: the construction of a machine which for example will 'cover' concerts will present no greater difficulties than the construction of an automatic chess player. The judgement of the accomplishment of the first meant machine, however, will present special difficulties which do not arise in the judgement of an automatic chess game.

Also in the investigation of an automatization of reasoning we can in the judgement of the accomplishments of a given 'thought machine' rely on well-described criteria. For the rest we are here, however, immediately in the middle of the problems to which modern studies into the foundations of mathematics thank, for an important part, their origins as well as their right to exist. In the sequel of the exposition this will become even more clear.

In any case we encounter here an extremely curious example of the eminently practical importance which afterwards clearly pertains to investigations which were initially instituted with purely theoretical intentions.

28. PREHISTORY

As to the *origin* of the conception of a 'thought machine' in the sense, described just now I would especially like to point out six points:

a. The analogy between calculating and reasoning must have been observed already in antiquity; this is evident from the following discussion of Aristotle.[1]

Because it is not possible in reasoning to deal with the objects themselves, but in their place we use words as symbols, we believe that what holds for the symbols holds also for the objects themselves, such as is the case with calculators and calculating stones.

But the comparison does not work because words and propositions are limited, and things themselves are infinite in number. It is therefore inevitable that one and the same expression and one and the same word denotes more than one object. Just as those who are inexperienced with the handling of the calculating stones are fooled by those who are experienced with them, so also do they miscalculate who are not informed of the portent of expressions and words, as well when they reason themselves as when they listen to others.

With even more emphasis Th. Hobbes calls upon this analogy in his *Leviathan*.[2]

b. The development, by Aristotle, of a doctrine of syllogism. I don't have to go more deeply into this point.[3]

c. The automatization of calculation, realized for the first time by B. Pascal in 1645.[4]

d. The formalization of logic, first demanded by G. W. Leibniz, but only very partially realized by him and his immediate followers. I have already dealt with this point.

e. The automatization of logical reasoning. Initial realizations of this conception, as the *Ars magna* of Raymundus Lullus (1236–1315), given new life by Ath. Kircher S. J. (1601–1680) in his *Ars magna sciendi* (Amsterdam, 1669), and the 'logical piano' of W. Stanley Jevons (1835–1882)[5], were doomed to remain 'playthings' as long as one did not have at his disposal a *complete* system of formalized logic.

f. The subsumption of calculating under logical reasoning as resulted from the logicistic foundation of mathematics according to F. Frege.[6]

29. DIFFICULTIES

The extremely wearisome course of affairs sketched in par. 28 has, of course, not been conducive to fruitful work in the construction of a 'thought machine'. It is true that one has already suspected for centuries that reasoning is bound by very rigorous rules comparable to the rules that govern counting and calculating, but the complete tracing of these rules presented insurmountable difficulties.

Aristotle, in his doctrine of syllogism, which I have already briefly mentioned, tracked down and described a number of these rules, the so-called *logical laws* or *laws of 'thought'*, and for this reason he is rightly known as the father of logic. His logic was, however, *incomplete*; it did not take into account a number of 'acts of thought', which, for example, can be indispensable in a mathematical proof. And one did not succeed directly in supplementing Aristotle's logistics in all these points. Naturally, in the long run, this did not stimulate confidence in formal logic and faith in the existence of rigorous 'laws of thought'.

As an example of the difficulties which one encounters, I mention the so-called *problem of Locke-Berkeley* which has had such great significance for the development of epistemology from Descartes to Kant. When in geometry one wants to prove a theorem valid for *all* triangles, then one usually fixes one's eye first on a particular triangle *ABC* and proves the theorem with regard to this triangle. Thereafter one says: the triangle *ABC* was chosen arbitrarily and so the theorem holds generally. In connection with this the following questions arise:

1. Why does one prove the theorem first for a particular triangle?

2. How can a reasoning which relates to a particular triangle nevertheless yield a result valid for all triangles?

Contemporary logic gives a conclusive answer to these questions which has been discussed amply in Chapter IV. But for centuries logicians have been at a loss with such questions. In this way in the long run the opinion originated according to which the expectation that reasoning would be governed by equally rigorous and well-determined laws as counting and calculating, had been an illusion.

30. DEVELOPMENT OF MODERN FORMAL LOGIC

Premature conclusions can lead a long life. Only around 1850 was there an earnest attempt to make a complete track-down, description and foundation of the laws of strict reasoning. This has led to often extremely laborious investigations which, however, finally have been crowned with complete success. By the completeness theorem of K. Gödel in 1930 it was established that we have at our disposal a *complete* description of logical reasoning in so far as it is of importance for the deductive construction of classical mathematics.

This description yields at the same time a reduction of argumentative thinking to a small number of elementary 'acts of thought' which are governed by simple laws comparable to the rules of calculation. As a characteristic example I mention the *modus ponens*:

$$\begin{array}{c} \textit{If U, then V} \\ U \\ \hline \therefore V \end{array}$$

31. AUTOMATIZATION OF REASONING

These theoretical results adjoined to the recent technological progress as to the construction and programming of progressively more powerful computers seem, in principle, to open up a road which in the long run could lead to the realization of the conception of a 'thought machine'.

Indeed since 1958 on the basis of work of S. Kanger and of myself, programs for electronic computers have been worked out by different investigators, which make it possible 'to order' machines in the execution of elementary logical deductions. I mention in this connection the work of B. Dunham, R. Fridshal and G. L. Sward (1959), of P. C. Gilmore (1959), of D. Prawitz, H. Prawitz and N. Voghera (1960) and of Hao Wang (1960).

A number of very simple deductions could be executed by the available machines. Even in the largest machines that exist at present the speed attainable is very low in comparison to what is needed for practical application.

32. ANALYSIS OF THE DIFFICULTIES

The design of an efficient 'thought machine' apparently still presents large difficulties, the grounds of which I wish to explore in broad outline. Each argumentation requires a relatively long sequence of 'acts of thought', and at each step one has to decide between a large number of possibilities. As the argumentation proceeds, the number of possibilities increases, and, moreover, the suitability of a choice once made can only be judged after some time.

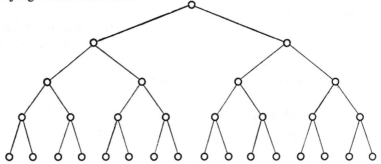

Whoever tries to present a mathematical proof seems to be looking for a road in a self-created maze; if one follows the good road, then one reaches the exit relatively quickly, but every side step complicates the maze. This consideration makes one comprehend both the fascinating effect of mathematics and the fear which it can create.

In this connection one has to mention A. Church's theorem (1936) which is a consequence of Gödel's famous *incompleteness* theorem (1931).

Gödel's earlier mentioned *completeness* theorem for predicate logic (1930) assures us that, if a sequent K/Z is valid, i.e., does not admit a counterexample, then this will become evident because the semantic tableau for that sequent closes. In this regard there is agreement with sentential logic.

In the last-mentioned case it is moreover true that if a sequent is *not* valid, the construction of the semantic tableau will bring this to light after a finite number of steps. In the case of sentential logic the construction of the semantic tableau therefore yields a decision procedure for the validity of a sequent.

According to Church's theorem, such a decision procedure cannot exist for predicate logic. This means that the construction of the semantic tableau can leave us in continual uncertainty as to the validity of a sequent K/Z. Such a sequent is then *not* valid (if it were valid, we would notice that because the semantic tableau would close), but from the course of the construction this will not become clear. If after a great number of steps closure is not yet attained, still this does not prove that continuation will not lead to closure. The possibility of such a situation indicates further that there can also be no principle which directs us in the maze described before. Such a guide post would lead to a decision procedure, and according to Church's theorem there can't be one.

33. AN EXAMPLE

A more concrete example may make things clearer. The solution of a geometric problem requires as a rule the drawing of a suitable auxiliary line. If one gives such a problem to a poor student, then he will draw an auxiliary line haphazardly. Usually the solution won't come out; and so, again haphazardly, a second auxiliary line is drawn, and so on. In less than no time the boy has a paper full of lines but no solution; he gives up or has to start anew. A good student, on the other hand, immediately draws the 'good' auxiliary line and the solution to the problem then usually smoothly appears. He 'sees' it, one usually says then.

I have presented the matter here really somewhat simpler than it is. In more difficult cases even the best pupil will not immediately make the best choice. Even then however he will go to work in a more efficient way than the poor student. In the first place he *'sees'* faster that his choice was incorrect, and in the second place he will also, on the basis of this insight, be directed to the right choice. Even in still more difficult cases, which require a patient investigation of different possibilities, he will know how to avoid useless detours. So he has, it seems, a guidepost in the maze, after all.

The good student knows each time to choose from the many logically admissable 'acts of thought' that one which brings him closer to the desired goal. The poor student, too, executes exclusively logically admissable 'acts of thought' (were he to transgress the logical laws then he would not be a poor, but a bad student), but he does not know how to choose these effectively.

34. HEURISTICS OR METHODOLOGY

A 'thought machine', too, not only has to abstain from logically in-admissable 'acts of thought', but moreover has to know at each time how to choose the most efficient 'act of thought'; otherwise its efficiency would be just as scanty as that of the poor student. We will therefore have to try to endow our machine with something which more or less corresponds to the *'insight'*, the guide-post of our good student. The realization of this idea is at the moment pursued in two manners.

In the first place one examines what the *'insight'* of the good student really consists of. This way one enters the realm of *thought psychology*, where, especially during the last decades, a lot of important work has been accomplished. I refer here to the publications of A. D. de Groot and J. Piaget.

By A. Newell and H. A. Simon (1956) and by H. Gelernter (1957), a connection has been made between thought-psychology and the treat-ment of the problems which are connected with the construction of a 'thought machine'. This work deserves to be strongly stimulated; ac-cording to my opinion one cannot expect complete clarification of a predominantly thought-psychologically founded *'heuristics'*.

In the second place one can remark that arithmetic has never restricted itself to the establisment of the fundamental rules for counting and calculation. It has soon put itself to the task of investigating more and more thoroughly the properties of numbers, and one has made grateful and intensive use of the so-acquired theoretical arithmetical insight both in practical calculating and in the construction of computers. So also *logic* shall not content itself with completely establishing the elementary 'laws of thought'. It will also have to endeavor to make available a more thorough knowledge of the properties of arguments which are constructed form elementary 'laws of thought'.

35. METHODOLOGY

Thus one comes to the development of a *metalogic, methodology* or logic in a wider sense. Since 1915 a number of important contributions have been made to this branch of science, also in connection with studies into mathematical foundations. I mention the *completeness theorems* of

L. Löwenheim (1915), Th. Skolem (1922) and K. Gödel (1930), the *deduction theorem* of J. Herbrand (1930) and of A. Tarski (1930), the theorems of J. Herbrand (1930) and of G. Gentzen (1934), my own results concerning the so-called method of Padoa (1953) and the *interpolation theorem* of W. Craig and R. C. Lyndon (1957).[7]

I already mentioned the *incompleteness theorem* of K. Gödel (1931) which implies the impossibility of a decision procedure for elementary arithmetic and, on the basis of Church's theorem, also for predicate logic. Curiously enough, on the other hand there is a decision procedure for elementary Euclidean geometry, as demonstrated by Tarski (1938).

For the construction of an efficient 'thought' or 'reasoning' machine, it will, however, not be sufficient to apply the results already available at present. It will also be necessary to achieve completely new theoretical results in the area of metalogic.

Notably I think in this connection of the characterization of the lemmas *Y* which can be 'interpolated' in an attempt to derive a certain conclusion *Z* from a certain premiss set *K*. For it is conceivable that, while the deduction problem K/Z exceeds the capacity of the machine, this is not the case with either of the problems K/Y and K/Z. A recent publication of W. Craig (1960) seems to open certain perspectives in this direction.

The investigations which in the long run will have to enable the construction of a 'thought machine' will therefore, in expectation thereof, even now stimulate both the development and the mutual interaction of thought psychology and metalogic, two branches of science which also on entirely different grounds would deserve much more attention than they usually get at present.

Even if it becomes evident that within the near future construction of an efficient 'thought machine' will not be possible, the work spent on the different research-projects in that direction must not all be fruitless.

36. CONCLUDING REMARKS

We can calmly refer the terror of a future conspiracy of 'thought machines' against humanity to the realm of 'science fiction' where it belongs. There is, however, a different ground for anxiety which I would like to bring to the reader's attention.

The automatization of calculation has not been the only practical fruit of the development of theoretical arithmetic. Another fruit was a method of teaching which has facilitated intellectual control to such an extent that it has finally become possible for everybody to learn how to calculate. This has undoubtedly contributed very greatly to the intellectual emancipation of broad layers of the people. If, though, the automatization of calculation had been brought about before the method of teaching meant here had become available, then knowledge of calculation would perhaps always have remained the privilege of an intellectual elite.

Logic now does not only serve the construction and investigation of mathematical and other deductive theories, it is moreover also a powerful expedient for rational critique. The creation and continuation of all kinds of philosophical and political systems is only possible owing to a great lack of command of logic, even in intellectual circles. In my opinion, this is mostly to be blamed on the absence of the indispensible method of teaching. As an illustration of this opinion may I refer to the numerous introductory tracts which have appeared in the last years. With all their good intentions, none of them succeeded in imparting to the reader what he needs; there is here also a *'threshold value'* which one has to exceed before the reader begins to perceive any useful effect.

The concentration of the attention of logicians on the theoretical aspects of the problems concerning the 'thought machine' should therefore not be detrimental to the development of a method of teaching which, at least for broad intellectual circles, brings within easy reach a minimum of knowledge and command of logic; this minimum is determined by the condition that the acquired logical knowledge can indeed yield a clearly demonstrable useful effect as expedient for rational critique.

NOTES

[1] Aristotle, *De sophisticis elenchis* 1.
[2] E. W. Beth [E²].
[3] J. Łukasiewicz [1].
[4] *L'œuvre de Pascal,* texte établi et annoté par J. Chevalier, Paris 1936.
[5] W. Stanley Jevons [1].
[6] E. W. Beth [H].
[7] E. W. Beth [W].

PART II

CHAPTER VI

THE PARADOXES

Just over half a century ago the scientific world was startled by the discovery of a number of paradoxes which formed a threat for the foundations of logic and mathematics. This discovery came completely unexpectedly and dealt a heavy blow to scientists like Cantor, Dedekind and Frege, who had made great efforts to achieve a foundation and construction of mathematics which would satisfy the strictest demands of logic.

Now that logicians have been familiar with the paradoxes, for more than half a century, they have recovered somewhat from the shock. They have even learned, as Henri Poincaré had already recommended, to take advantage of the situation. I hope in the following to give an impression of the fruits that the investigation of the paradoxes has reaped for logic.

To confine the thoughts, I will first give a survey of the paradoxes in the order of their appearance. Afterwards I want to discuss some characteristic cases in detail, and finally I hope to say something about the solution of the pardoxes. Enumeration of the Paradoxes:

(1) The paradox of the Liar, which was known already in Antiquity;

(2) The paradox of C. Burali-Forti (1897), which disturbed Cantor as early as 1895;

(3) The paradox of B. Russell (1903), at the same time also remarked by E. Zermelo;

(4) The paradox of J. Richard (1905);

(5) The paradox of Zermelo-König (1905);

(6) The paradox of denotation (Russell 1905);

(7) The paradox of G. G. Berry (published by Russell in 1906);

(8) The paradox of K. Grelling (1908);

(9) The (pseudo-) paradox of the barber (Russell 1918);

(10) The paradox of Th. Skolem (1923);

(11) The paradox of the largest cardinal number, discovered by Cantor in 1899, but published only (with his correspondence) after his death (1932).

Russell's paradox appears if we state the following definition relying on the axiom of comprehension[1]:

(a) *Let R be the set of all sets which do not contain themselves as an element.* In other words:

(b) For every x: x belongs to R, if and only if x does not belong to x. If we apply (b) for R as a particular value of x, then we obtain:

(c) *R belongs to R, if and only if R does not belong to R.*

With this we have reached the paradox. For, (d) if R belongs to R, then R does *not* belong to R, and (e) if R does *not* belong to R, then R belongs to R.

This paradox lends itself well to a formulation by means of logical symbols. In order to express that x is contained as an element in the set y, we use the formula:

$$y(x).$$

The definition of R, as formulated in (b), is then represented by the formula:

(b_0) $(x)\,[R(x)\leftrightarrow\overline{x(x)}],\, x(x)],$

from which immediately follows:

(c_0) $R(R)\leftrightarrow\overline{R(R)},$

(d_0) $R(R)\rightarrow\overline{R(R)},$

(e_0) $\overline{R(R)}\rightarrow R(R).$

The *Berry paradox* is a simplified form of the Richard paradox, which in its turn is closely related to the paradox of Zermelo-König. We assume as given a sufficient English language vocabulary (such a vocabulary, for example, as might be obtained by making a list of all words and symbols used in this article). This vocabulary will contain only a *finite* number of words. We consider all sentences formed by means of at most 50 words or symbols which all must be taken from our vocabulary. These sentences, too, are finite in number. Among all these sentences we consider in particular those which define a natural number. These last sentences *a fortiori* form a finite set C and the set N of the numbers so-defined will likewise be finite. There must therefore be natural numbers which do not belong to N, and which therefore cannot be defined by means of a sentence belonging to C. Under these natural numbers, there must be a smallest one; this smallest natural number which does not belong to N is denoted as the *Berry number*. Now let us consider the following sentence:

The Berry number is the smallest natural number which cannot be defined by means of a sentence containing at most 50 words, all of them taken from our vocabulary.

This sentence contains only 30 words and symbols, all of which occur in our vocabulary; it defines a natural number, in fact the Berry number. The sentence considered belongs to *C* and therefore the natural number defined by it belongs to *N*. For that reason the Berry number belongs to *N*, while initially it was described as the smallest natural number not belonging to *N*. So again we encounter a paradox.

To avoid the paradoxes one has recommended different procedures. According to Brouwer, a part of classical mathematics has lost the essential and indispensable content with the living reality of the intuitive mathematical thought which is constructive and independent of logic; this part of classical mathematics lacks an object which can be constructed from the original mathematical intuition. A return to the natural starting point of mathematical thought and an adaptation of mathematical language to mathematical thoughts should be sufficient to allow us to overcome the paradoxes; the development of intuitionistic mathematics by Brouwer and Heyting has confirmed this expectation.

Also the axiomatization of Cantor's set theory by E. Zermelo, A. A. Fraenkel, Th. Skolem, J. von Neumann, P. Bernays and K. Gödel has led to the elimination of the paradoxes; in this case one does not have to renounce familiar methods and results of classical (i.e. non-intuitionistic) mathematics.

To judge the respective merits of intuitionism and of axiomatic set-theory one should, however, not only pay attention to the results reached with regard to the problem created by the occurrence of the paradoxes. On the other hand this problem exceeds the domain where the discussion between intuitionism and set theory takes place; the paradoxes threaten in the first place the foundations of logic, and so they should be considered mainly from the standpoint of general logic.

Russell has tackled the problem of the paradoxes with the aid of purely logical methods. He initially experimented with the *theory of limitation of size*, the *zigzag theory*, the *no-class theory*, and the *theory of logical types*. The first theory found to a certain extent a further elaboration in the continued development of Zermelo's axiomatization, the second found a counterpart much later in Quine's *New Foundations*, while the third, at closer range, turned out not to be esentially different from the fourth. Thus in 1908 Russell published a logical system based on the theory of types; I will merely render here some of the main features.

The theory of types desubstantializes classes to a certain extent and subjects them to a hierarchy. Besides the individual objects represented by the variables $x_0, y_0, z_0, \ldots$ of *type zero*, there are classes of individual objects represented by the variables $x_1, y_1, z_1, \ldots$ of *type one*, classes of classes, represented by the variables $x_2, y_2, z_2, \ldots$ of *type two*, classes of classes of classes, represented by the variables $x_3, y_3, z_3, \ldots$ of *type three*, and so on. Only (atomic) formulas like $y_1(x_0), x_2(x_1), z_3(y_2), \ldots$ are therefore meaningful; formulas like $y_0(x_1), x_2(x_2), z_3(y_1), \ldots$ are not meaningful and are therefore not admitted. It is easy to see that, for example, the Russell paradox is avoided in this way.

Nevertheless general acceptance of the theory of types turns out to be foiled mainly because of two difficulties. In the first place many logicians consider the theory of types as an artificial, *ad hoc* measure. I would, however, like to point out the distinction made by Aristotle[2] between individual objects as *primary* substances and species as *secondary* substances, which can be considered as a first step to the theory of types. The fact that one can also find an anticipation of the theory of types in Schröder[3] likewise indicates the natural character of the theory of types.

In the second place acceptance of the theory of types does not suit the integral program of logicism, which demands a deduction of pure mathematics exclusively on the basis of the principles of pure logic. It is true that such a deduction, already desired by Leibniz, had been accomplished by Frege but the principles he appealed to, notable the unrestricted *axiom of comprehension*, later turned out to give rise to paradoxes.

When Whitehead and Russell, in their *Principia Mathematica*[4], tried to reconstruct Frege's deduction in accordance with the theory of types, it turned out that they needed not only the axiom of comprehension, now restricted in its range of application, but also the so-called *axiom of infinity*. In contrast to the axiom of comprehension, the axiom of infinity has a specific mathematical character.

Logicians have not resigned themselves to this unsatisfactory state of affairs. Especially the logicists under them have continued the attempts to construct a '*logica magna*', a system of pure logic that has to encompass the whole of pure mathematics. For that one requires a relaxation of the restrictions resulting from the theory of types; this relaxation has to be radical enough to enable the accomplisment of the integral program of logicism; it cannot go so far that the chance for new paradoxes exists.

In the investigations, to which these problems have led, there are three aspects to be distinguished, namely:

(1) The construction of new logical systems to replace the system of *Principia Mathematica*.

(2) Closer investigation of the 'mechanism' which in certain logical or deductive systems (notably in Frege's pure logic and in Cantor's set theory) causes the paradoxes.

(3) Analysis of the individual paradoxes.

Regarding point (1) I mention in the first place W. V. Quine's *New Foundations* (1937) and *Mathematical Logic* (1940). This last system turned out to lead to paradoxes, (R. C. Lyndon 1941, J. B. Rosser 1941), but a new version (1951) appeared free of contradictions, thanks to a correction indicated by Hao Wang. Quine makes use of certain ideas, derived from axiomatic set theory. On the other hand Th. Skolem (1922), A. A. Fraenkel (1922–1928), J. von Neumann (1923–1929), P. Bernays (1937–1948) and K. Gödel (1940), starting from the work of Zermelo, have solidified the logical structure of the axiomatic set theory and made it more transparent. It hardly makes sense any more to make a distinction between logicism and cantorism.

Regarding point (2) I mention, to start with, the remark made by H. Behmann (1931), that the definitions which lead to the different paradoxes have a special character: they don't satisfy the requirement already put forward by Pascal that each definition has to enable us to replace the defined term by its definiens.

Indeed, if, for example in the case of the Russell paradox, we attempt this replacement of the defined term 'R' in the formula '$R(R)$' then we obtain the formula '$\overline{R(R)}$' which still contains the defined term 'R'.

The importance of Behmann's remark lies in the fact that only for definitions which satisfy Pascal's condition it is determined without proof that their introduction can never cause the occurrence of a paradox. So it is obvious to assume that the occurrence of the Russell paradox in Frege's system should not be ascribed to the contradictory nature of Frege's system itself, but to the introduction of a definition which does not satisfy Pascal's condition. That this assumption is right was proved later by the Russian mathematician D. A. Bochvar (1944).

This result sheds more light on the role of the axiom of comprehension. It is this axiom that justifies the introduction of definitions which do not satisfy Pascal's condition. We can avoid the paradoxes by accepting suitable restrictions as to the introduction of definitions which do not satisfy Pascal's condition or, what amounts to the same thing, as to the application of the axiom of comprehension. The earlier mentioned systems of Russell and Quine, as well as the axiomatizations of set theory by Skolem, Fraenkel, von Neumann and their followers, are without exception characterized by such restrictions. We have already seen that these restrictions should not go too far. –

Under point (2) also falls the fundamental distinction between *logical* and *semantical* paradoxes. Working from a remark already made by G. Peano, F. P. Ramsey (1926) directed attention to the fact that, if one formalizes logic and mathematics in the usual way, some paradoxes [notably the numbers (2), (3), and (11)] can be formulated by means of formalized language, while others [notably numbers (1) and (4)–(8)] can not go along with this step and "stay behind" in a commentary on the formal system formulated by means of normal text.

The introduction to Russell's theory of types only influences the formal system and leads directly only to the elimination of the paradoxes of the first kind (Ramsey's 'Group A', now denoted as logical paradoxes); the paradoxes of the second kind ('Group B', the semantical paradoxes) are not directly influenced by the theory of types. Ramsey rightly concludes from this that certain complications which Russell included in his theory of types just for the sake of avoiding the semantical paradoxes are superfluous; naturally since then the original so-called 'ramified' version of the theory of types has made way for a simplified 'non-ramified' version.[5]

As I have already discussed the Russell paradox rather in detail as the simplest example of a logical paradox, I now want to discuss, by way of illustration of (3), the analysis of the Berry paradox as the simplest example of a semantical paradox.

We ask ourselves what happens to this paradox if we formalize arithmetic by means of a formal system A in which only a finite number of elementary symbols are used. The introductory considerations given above are still valid, except for some small modifications. So we can immediately draw up the following definition:

The Berry number for the system A is the smallest natural number which cannot be defined by means of a formula of the system A consisting of at most fifty elementary symbols.

In the first place we remark that the paradox has vanished; indeed there is no contradiction between the observations:

1. The Berry number for the system A is the smallest natural number which cannot be defined by means of a formula of the system A consisting of at most 50 elementary symbols, and:

2. The Berry number for the system A can be defined by means of a sentence of everyday language consisting of 32 words.

Somewhat more thorough considerations, however, lead to conclusions of a much wider scope. Let us imagine that we could 'translate' the above definition into the system A and that as a result of this 'translation' a formula B_{50} of the system A is obtained. Then B_{50} is a definition of the Berry number for the system A, and according to observation 1, B_{50} should therefore consist of 51 or more elementary symbols. That in itself, of course, is not surprising; we can very well imagine that the 'translation' of a sentence consisting of 32 words yields a somewhat verbose formula B_{50} of the system A. Let us assume for the sake of argument that B_{50} consists of 73 elementary symbols.

We replace the word '*fifty*' in the above definition with the word '*one thousand*'; the Berry number then, of course, changes, while in observation 1 one has to read instead of '50 *elementary symbols*', now '1000 *elementary symbols*'. On the basis of this observation a 'translation' B_{1000} of the new definition should consist of at least 1001 elementary symbols; on the other hand B_{1000} is of course obtained when we replace the notation for the number 50 according to the system A by the corresponding notation for the number 1000.

The fact that the number of elementary symbols thereby increases from 73 to 1001 (or more) is perhaps surprising, but not completely unthinkable. It is imaginable that the notation of the natural numbers according to the formal system A is particularly verbose, if we assume however that the system A disposes of a reasonably compact notation for the natural numbers, then an increase from 73 to 1001 (or more) is *indeed* inconceivable.

To see this let us hold ourselves to the numbers just mentioned, and we assume also that in the system A the usual notation for natural numbers remains in force. Because the numbers '5' and '0' each count for *one* elementary symbol, the formula B_{50} can at most contain 36 times the combination of the figures '50'. Then the formula B_{1000} will also contain at most 36 times the combination of figures '1000', and for the rest exactly the same symbols which also occur in B_{50}, so that B_{1000} will consist of at most 145 elementary symbols. But according to the modified observation (1) B_{1000} should contain at least 1001 elementary symbols, and we have to obtain the contradiction.

We therefore have to conclude that the supposed 'translations' B_{50} and B_{1000} cannot exist, in other words, that the definitions in question are not susceptible to 'translation' in the system A. Further reflection gives us the insight that the difficulty must be situated in the concept of *definition* to the extent that this pertains to the connection between a defining sentence (or formula) and the natural number defined by it (A. Tarski, 1931).

In an analogous way the analysis of the paradox of the Liar produces the insight that there exists a difficulty as to the matter of the concept of *truth* to the extent that this pertains to the connection between a sentence (or formula) and the state of affairs expressed by it. A formal system A (which fulfills certain conditions which won't be discussed further here) cannot adequately express the concepts *definition* and *truth* with regard to the formulas of the system A itself. With the paradoxes named under (4)–(6) and (8), of which the analysis given by Tarski demonstrated that formal systems are also inadequate with respect to other semantical notions (I mention in particular the notions *meaning* and *denotation*); one often denotes at present the numbers (1) and (7) as *semantical paradoxes*.

Tarski designates a formal system A as discussed above as *semantically not closed*, because it does not yield an adequate formulation of its own semantics. Such a formal system differs in this point from everyday language which yields an adequate formulation of its own semantics and which Tarski on these grounds designates as *semantically closed*. In my opinion he has shown convincingly that the semantical paradoxes result from the semantical closedness of everyday language.[6]

NOTES

[1] Comp. p. 89.
[2] Aristotle, *De praedicamentis* 5, 2ª, 11.
[3] Comp. A. Church [1].
[4] A. N. Whitehead and B. Russell [1].
[5] Comp. E. W. Beth [U].
[6] A. Tarski [1], [4]; comp. B. H. Kazemier [1], G. Nuchelmans [2], E. W. Beth [107ª].

CHAPTER VII

REASON AND INTUITION

About the Curious Character of Our Logical and Mathematical Knowledge in Connection with the Struggle between Nominalism and Platonism

1. The struggle between nominalism and platonism is practically as old as philosophy itself.[1] What is at stake is the meaning which has to be attached to general terms as '*good*', '*red*', or '*horse*'. According to platonism such a general term denotes a substance just as much as a particular term or proper name (for example '*Napoleon*' or '*Schreierstoren*'), even if it is a substance of a very particular ideal non-material nature. Nominalism objects to the existence of such ideal individual substances; it conceives of a general term as a collective denotation for a multiplicity of individual substances, and so tries to avoid an appeal to ideal substances or abstract entities. Platonism does not go so far (except for extreme forms)[2] as to deny the multiplicity of the individual substances characterized by a general term, but deems the unity of denotation inexplicable without the assumption of a substantial unity in or behind this multiplicity.

We are faced here with a question of which the discussion seems to be able to lead merely to an exchange of subtleties without firm foundation and which should therefore be counted to the so-called pseudo-problems; curiously enough, however, modern foundational studies have led to a resumption of the debate about the problem of *universalia*. In order to make the situation completely clear, we must first stand still for a moment and look at modern foundational studies more in general. Even earlier there has been the need for a clarification of the fundamental principles of the different areas of science; nevertheless modern foundational studies differ from earlier attempts in this direction in a characteristic way.

2. The validity of the fundamental principles of the different branches of science was not seriously questioned in the past. On the contrary,

between philosophers and practitioners of the sciences there existed an unanimity which made possible a certain division of labor: the scientific investigator could accept the principles of his area as an unassailable starting point; so the philosopher left it to him to investigate his areas as thoroughly as possible and merely applied himself to investigating the principles of each area, to comparing the principles of different areas, to determining their mutual connections, to reducing them to each other and especially to explaining the origin of our knowledge of these principles; the philosopher did not have to concern himself with the progress of scientific investigation, because the certainty of the principles could never be undermined by this.

When, from time to time, the philosophers in their analytic work came to discuss the validity of the principles, then it was in no way the intention to revise the foundations of some branch or other of science. The methodical doubt of Descartes, the epoch of Husserl, have a purely academic character; one does not look for a new foundation of science, one strives to form a firmer conviction concerning the correctness of the principles of an already existing science. The skeptics tried to undermine certain rational convictions, to replace these by a form of contemplation which goes far above any scientific insight. With other thinkers the doubt as to the validity of the principle of the excluded third, or the law of causality, does not in so much regard the application of these principles in logic or natural sciences as its extension to other areas as theology or psychology.

Since the first decade of the 19th century this situation has changed completely; the development of the sciences themselves has led to imminent critique of their principles, the so-called foundational crisis. In logic this foundational crisis has given rise to new discussions over the problem of *universalia*.[3]

3. Between 1880 and 1900 G. Frege (1848–1925) and G. Cantor (1845–1918) have independently of each other endeavoured to derive pure mathematics in its entirety from a small number of simple and evident principles. With Frege these principles belonged to general logic (which, in his set-up, includes the whole of pure mathematics), while Cantor derives his principles from his own set theory, a mathematical theory which is by its abstract and general character closely related to general

logic. In themselves, these aspirations of Frege and Cantor were not incompatible with traditional conceptions. The novelty lies mainly in the
fact that the individual systems of principles for arithmetic, geometry,
etc. are replaced by one single system and that this system, as well with
Frege as with Cantor, is much simpler and much more evident than each
of the individual systems assumed before. Neither Frege nor Cantor
questioned the validity of the principles for arithmetic, geometry, etc.
summed up in these systems; they aimed – without doubt also on the
basis of philosophical considerations – at a unification of pure mathematics and a simplification of its foundations, but this did not mean a break
with traditional conceptions concerning mathematics and its principles.

4. The discovery of the paradoxes of logic and set theory, as is well
known, made both the construction of pure mathematics given by Cantor
and that by Frege untenable.[4] One therefore either had to abandon the
idea of a unification of pure mathematics, or to subject the systems of
Frege and Cantor to a basic revision. As an introduction to our considerations about nominalism, we shall presently discuss some attempts at
revision, after first having concluded our general exposition.

The systems of basic principles for logic and set theory one has formulated to replace Frege's and Cantor's systems completely lack the
simplicity and the evidence of these systems. This development is characteristic for modern foundational studies, which is not only directed by
philosophical considerations, but also very closely connected with the
sciences. The division of labor sketched above between philosophy and
the sciences consequently cannot be maintained. The validity of the
principles of the distinct areas of the sciences (in our case of logic and set
theory) can no longer be deemed unassailable, and in judging them one
should not only take into account philosophical considerations, but also
results from these sciences.

5. We want to stand still for a moment with the necessity of a practically
complete revision of these principles, since the practice of speculative
philosophy is different in this respect. If, to name an example, at a certain
moment in a deductively constructed speculative system a difficulty
arises – for example, an inner-contradiction, or an objection which is
difficult to obviate – then one often introduces an *ad hoc* revision: an
earlier given description of a concept is made more precise (often by the

introduction of a new distinction), or an earlier accepted principle is supplied with a new restrictive condition.

After this one demonstrates that the inner-contradiction is obviated or that the objection is now refutable; usually, however, one does not investigate whether the previous part of the argument keeps its validity after the introduction of the revision.

In a deductive argument, which wants to satisfy the requirements put by contemporary methodology, such an *ad hoc revision* is completely inadmissible, however; after the introduction of the necessary modifications of the principles one should test the validity of the whole argument once more.

It turns out that if one is serious in living up to the postulates of a rigorous methodology, then the introduction of a suitable revision usually presents ticklish problems: in the first place the revision has to be radical enough to give a solution for the difficulties; on the other hand, however, it should not affect the validity of the argument.

6. We can now proceed with the discussion of the principles drawn up by Frege and Cantor, and of the revision to be introduced therein. One can say that the main principle of both Frege and Cantor was the so-called *axiom of comprehension*[7], which I will formulate in terms of set theory: (i) mathematical entities which have a certain property in common form a *set* of which they are the *elements* and which is unambiguously determined by the property in question; (ij) each set is a mathematical entity and so in its turn can occur as an element of a set; (iij) sets which contain the same elements are identical.

This axiom of comprehension (to which Frege also appeals, although its formulation is different in logic) has a high measure of simplicity, evidence and naturalness. These characteristics also apply to the few principles which Cantor and Frege still need as supplementation. Moreover it is certain that both these investigators have been able to derive the whole of pure mathematics from the principles accepted by them (without appealing to specific arithmetical, specific geometrical,... axioms). But alas, it is also certain that the axiom of comprehension in the original form given just now leads to paradoxes and therefore cannot yield a tenable foundation.[4]

7. In the attempts to revise the axiom of comprehension, (in which, on

the one hand, the paradoxes have to be avoided, and, on the other hand, the possibility of the derivation of the whole of pure mathematics has to be maintained) one can distinguish two main directions which consecutively go back to Russell and Zermelo. Russell mainly builds on Frege; Zermelo mainly on Cantor, but a sharp boundary cannot be drawn; Quine's work, for example, joins up as well with the tradition of Cantor-Zermelo as that of Frege-Russell.[8]

Zermelo's theory admits only *one* type of mathematical entities, which are designated as *sets*. This designation, which at first sight can create confusion, expresses that these entities are on the one hand recognized as individuals, to which for that reason some properties can be given, but on the other hand can contain elements, and so also are to be considered as multiplicities. Sets which have a certain property in common form a *class*; in general such a class is only recognized as a multiplicity, and therefore not as a mathematical entity. Classes which fulfill certain conditions (not to be discussed here) can, however, be 'compressed'[9] to sets and therefore are recognized as a mathematical entity; these conditions are described in a new axiom of comprehension.

The difference between the two axioms of comprehension (in the old axiom one should for the sake of comparison replace the term 'set' by the term 'class') apparently regards clause (ij), which in the new terminology would be as follows: (ij^0) each class is a set and can therefore in its turn occur as an element of a class. If we would take up clause (ij^0) in Zermelo's theory, then it would distinguish itself only terminologically from the theory of Cantor and would therefore equally lead to paradoxes. Zermelo for that reason includes in his axiom of comprehension a more restrictive clause (ij*), which only allows a 'compression' to sets of classes which fulfill certain conditions; it indeed turns out to be possible to choose these conditions in such a way that the compression remains possible in all these cases where it is required for the construction of Cantor's theory, but is excluded in those cases, in which it would lead to paradoxes.

(By way of illustration I mention the solution to the Russell paradox: on the basis of clause (i), in the new terminology, the sets which do not contain themselves as an element form a well-determined class; but clause (ij*) does not allow us to compress this class to a set, so that the paradox is abrogated; in this connection we remark rather superfluously that only sets can occur as an element of a class.)

Russell's so-called theory of types introduces a hierarchy in the mathe-matical entities; there are entities of type 0, of type 1, of type 2, etc. Entities of one and the same type, which have a certain property in common, form a class; it is true that such a class is recognized as a mathematical entity, but it is in type one number higher than its elements. In this case the revision concerns clause (i) of the old axiom of compre-hension.

Like Cantor, Zermelo and Russell also need, besides (a) the axiom of comprehension, some supplementary principles, which we don't have to discuss in more detail, but which we will mention for the sake of complete-ness: (b) axioms for the sentential calculus; (c) axioms for the theory of quantification; (d) axioms of extensionality; (e) axioms of choice; (f) an axiom of infinity.

8. The platonistic tendency in Russell's as well as Zermelo's theory is un-deniable. With Russell, besides the individuals (entities of type 0), there occur also entities 'of higher order' (type 1, type 2, ...) which, although they are distinguished from the individuals, are still treated in a completely analogous way. These entities of higher order strongly remind us of Plato's ideas, with this understanding that with Russell also the 'ideas' are again subjected to a hierarchy.

In Zermelo there is a platonic trait, in the possibility of, under certain circumstances, compressing a class which in the first instance has been given as a multiplicity to a unity (a set).

Of still greater significance, however, is the fact that the axiom of comprehension makes possible *impredicative definitions*, both with Zermelo and Russell. Such an impredicative definition characterizes a mathematical entity while referring to a class to which this entity itself belongs. In Russell's theory such a definition can be recognized from the fact that the definiens either mentions an entity which is of a higher type than the definiendum, or contains a quantifier which ranges over entities of equal or higher type.[10]

To see the curious character of this kind of definition we take for a moment a genetic point of view. Obviously we then start to generate the entities of type 0 (individuals). Next we can start classifying individuals in all possible ways, by which we obtain classes of individuals, i.e. entities of type 1. By now classifying these new entities in all possible ways we obtain classes of classes (of individuals) i.e. entities of type 2 etc. In this genesis the entities of higher type appear later than those of lower type. The introduction of an entity by means of an impredicative definition clearly means an infringement on the 'natural' genetic order sketched here. For this definition refers to a class to which the entity to be introduced belongs itself, and which therefore can only come into existence after the entity to be introduced has itself already been obtained.

For the platonist, of course, impredicative definitions present no difficulties. For him the genetic order sketched just now can have no other than a perhaps even doubtful heuristic value; the whole system of individuals, classes of individuals, classes of classes, etc. is for him already present before he starts his investigation. A definition can therefore never serve to create a new entity, but only to put forward from the stock already available one definite entity; and impredicative definitions can serve this purpose just as well as predicative. By way of example I mention: '*Plato is the greatest Greek thinker*'. If, for the moment, we overlook a possible difference of opinion with regard to the relative significance of the Greek thinkers, we can consider this proposition as a definition of Plato, because it unambiguously characterizes in the class of all Greek thinkers one definite thinker, notably the greatest one, namely Plato; this definition, of course, does not intend to add another new element to the class of all Greek thinkers, it merely puts forward one definite element from this class.

Nevertheless there is every indication to view the impredicative definitions and platonism with some suspicion because – as especially Poincaré and Russell argued – the paradoxes are also based on impredicative definitions, so that their occurrence can easily be charged to the platonic inspiration of Frege and Cantor. Now it is true that the revision of the axiom of comprehension according to Zermelo and Russell makes those impredicative definitions impossible, which led to the paradoxes, but it did not lead to a radical prohibition of this kind of definitions. Such a prohibition would also have made the unification of pure mathematics, aspired for by Zermelo and Russell, impossible, since impredicative definitions play an important role in the proof of classical results like the theorem of the least upper bound in the theory of real numbers, and the theorem of Cantor about the uncountability of the continuum, which by far the most mathematicians would not readily abandon.[11]

9. The reactions to the situation, created by the construction of the theories of Zermelo and Russell, in which the platonistic element was hardly less clear than with Frege and Cantor were extremely divergent.

Some investigators saw little good in continuing the unification attempts of Frege and Cantor and preferred to link up with the mathematics of a somewhat earlier period; thus originated intuitionism and formalism, about which, at present, I don't have to say much. Among those who advocated continuation of the unification policy we can distinguish two main streams.

The *platonists* – I mention A. Church, K. Gödel, and H. Scholz – can view the situation with tranquillity. According to them, Cantor's and Frege's aspirations were in principle right, and these thinkers just began with a too simplistic conception about the "universe of ideas", as became clear from the occurrence of the paradoxes. That one cannot derive from this an argument against platonism as such is obvious from the fact that Russell and Zermelo have been able to carry through their revision without a radical break with platonism.

10. The *nominalists*[12], on the other hand, ascribe the difficulties which seem to hamper the unification of pure mathematics to the platonistic element in the theories of Frege and Cantor, and the revisions made by Russell and Zermelo are therefore for them not in the least satisfactory. This tendency is already clearly demonstrable in Russell himself, but stands out more sharply in the work of L. Chwistek, S. Léśniewski, W. V. Quine, N. Goodman, L. Henkin and others; Tarski also takes a nominalistic standpoint, as became clear this summer in Amersfoort.[13]

If one wants to give form to the nominalistic aspirations, then in the first place an attempt must be made to replace the theories of Russell and Zermelo by a new theory, which does not have to appeal to platonistic conceptions like compression and the introduction of entities of higher order. Now an appeal to such conceptions is almost inevitable, if, as a basic concept one chooses the *inherence-* or *appartenance-relation*, the relation of an individual to a class to which it belongs. One must therefore try to replace this relation by a different basic concept. Goodman and Quine[14] have chosen as a basic concept the relation of part to whole, but it is doubtful if with this a suitable foundation for the whole of pure mathematics is given.

For that reason it looks very probable that, if the nominalists keep striving for a unification of pure mathematics in which classical results like the theorem of the least upper-bound are not abandoned, very little could be detracted from the theories of Zermelo and Russell.[15] From this it seems to follow, that the endeavor of the nominalists is doomed to failure.

11. In spite of that there remains a way out for the nominalists. Namely, one can try first to construct pure mathematics in the manner indicated by Russell and Zermelo, and then afterwards to interpret the so-obtained 'platonistically sounding' system in a nominalistic sense. Such an '*Als Ob*'-standpoint seems like Columbus' egg and initially inspires little confidence, but for all that there are different considerations which indicate its tenability.

We will first give a closer description of this nominalistic interpretation, and after that go into the question to what extent it is tenable.[16]

To begin with, we identify Russell's individuals with objects of a more-precisely-to-be-determined species S^1; in Zermelo the identification of his sets with objects of the species S^1 is less obvious, but we still accept it and respond to the objection that a set should be interpreted as a multiplicity by pointing to Zermelo's rather unfortunate use of the term 'set'. Taking into account the axiom of infinity, accepted by both Russell and Zermelo, we establish that S^1 has to contain countably many objects.

Before we proceed to the interpretation of the classes (of individuals or of sets), we determine that we will only recognize definable classes. Let us imagine for a moment a suitable definition written down for each definable class, then we see that there are countably many possible definitions, and therefore also countably many definable classes; so we can identify classes with objects of a new species S^2, provided S^2 contains countably many objects.

With this we are done with regard to Zermelo's theory. In Russell, it's now the turn for classes of classes. We again only recognize definable classes of classes, of which there are also countably many; we identify these with the objects of a new countable species S^3. In the same way we identify classes of classes of classes with the objects of a countable species S^4. And so on.

If we take the species S^1 and S^2 (respectively the species $S^1, S^2, S^3, \ldots$)

together, we get a new all-inclusive species S. The objects of the species S we can now identify with the *material bodies*, appealing to a '*cosmological hypothesis*', according to which the universe contains countably many material bodies.

12. We now indicate some difficulties which are connected with the proposed interpretation. In the first place it follows from the Richard paradox that the assumption according to which every class is definable is incompatible with the axioms on which Zermelo and Russell base themselves, if one takes the term 'definable' in the usual sense of "definable with the aid of an expression consisting of a finite number of words (or symbols)". Gödel has pointed out however that this difficulty is negated if one takes the term in a different sense, described by him with all desired accuracy.[17]

Further it follows from the theorem of Cantor mentioned in par. 8 that, if there are countably many individuals there have to be uncountably many classes; in the case of Russell's theory the required 'power' even rises with the number of the type considered. The class S would therefore have to have an uncountable power, while it wouldn't do to postulate, by means of a 'cosmological hypothesis' the existence of an uncountable power. This difficulty can be solved by referring to the paradox of Skolem-Löwenheim; if (for example) Zermelo's theory is free of contradiction, then according to Gödel it will remain free of contradiction after the addition of the supposition according to which all classes are definable in the manner meant by him; the so-supplemented theory can then be interpreted by means of a countable species S in which, then, also the species S^1 and S^2 will be countable. Now, contrary to Cantor's theorem, the power of S^2 is not greater than that of S^1, but this only holds if we consider the species S as part of a sufficiently more extensive species T; therefore the comparison of powers has a relative character, and this is exactly what one learns from the paradox of Skolem-Löwenheim. A similar argument holds with regard to Russell's theorem.

Finally one can make the objection that we may now have an interpretation of the individuals (i.e. sets) occurring with Russell and Zermelo, but that with this no interpretation has been given yet of the inherence- or appartenance-relation, which consequently remains suspended in an 'universe of ideas'. The answer to this is that this relation on the basis of the interpretation is 'demoted' to a relation between material bodies, and therefore comes to the same level with relations as '*heavier than*', '*touching*', which play a role in all kinds of empirical sciences.

13. Naturally one can object to the appeal to a cosmological hypothesis as mentioned above; its necessity resulted from the acceptance of the axiom of infinity. A similar difficulty already arises with regard to elementary arithmetic, and we can adopt the solution given for this case.[18] Let X be the axiom of infinity and A a theorem of Zermelo's theory (respectively Russell's) in the proof of which axiom X plays a role. According to the *deduction theorem*, the theorem: '*if X then A*' can then be proved in the theory in question without having to make an appeal to axiom X. We can therefore leave the axiom of infinity out provided we give to all theorems in the proof of which it plays a role the hypothetical form just indicated. For all practical purposes '*if X then A*' is just as useful to us as A.

The interpretation given above remains tenable now, but we can leave open the question of how many material objects the universe contains.

We observe that after the omission of the axiom of infinity the consistency of the theories of Zermelo and Russell can easily be proved.

14. That the nominalistic interpretation of the different forms of contemporary set theory is *tenable* can hardly be disputed after the above. But this does not mean that one has to accept this interpretation as the most suitable. Our judgement concerning that will depend strongly on personal considerations and on our philosophy and view of life; the one person will strongly tend to nominalism, the other to platonism. I once again leave the stage to both parties.

The platonist will observe, that it is true that the nominalistic interpretation of set theory is tenable, but also, to a high degree, artificial. By way of illustration he will refer to the replacement of the normal concept of definability by Gödel's, to the appeal to the paradox of Skolem-Löwenheim and to the hypothetical formulation of the theorems of set theory. Furthermore he will put forward that the nominalist fails to appreciate the intuition which has enabled the construction of set theory. If one abandons the conviction about the correctness of the insight, which finds expression in the axiom of infinity, then the theorems based on it become trivial. Cantor and the others were completely impressed with this insight, and the fact that they possessed such an insight cannot be explained unless one assumes that this intuition has a real foundation; in this last consideration one recognizes the ontological argument.

To counter this the nominalist will put forward that the influence of platonism on the creation of set theory is no proof for the correctness of platonism. It does explain the platonistic tendency, also in the newer versions of set theory. That the nominalistic interpretation of such a theory is artificial is not surprising. Important, however, is that it is possible; for this implies that one can accept, practice and apply set theory, without simultaneously accepting platonism.

15. In the light of these considerations, lastly, I want to dedicate a few words to the question, which mode of cognition is responsible for our knowledge of the principles of logic and mathematics.

This question is deemed by many as unfit for discussion. One means with that, then, that the question involves certain concepts and points of view which are incapable of being specified to such an extent as is needed in order to come to a response binding to all competent critics. Indeed such concepts and points of view will play a role in the following; in my opinion this does not imply that the discussion of the question raised here could not be fruitful, but only that we (i) cannot have the pretension to prove the correctness of our response, and (ij) cannot require that one should wait with the treatment of less speculative problems until a satisfactory answer to our question is obtained.

I observe now already, that terms like 'knowing' and 'cognition' should be used w th great circumspection, but before I go into this point I will recall some conceptions on the nature of logico-mathematical knowledge.

(Ia)   The intuitionist conceives of it as a form of self-knowledge.

(Ib)   The formalist can among other ways conceive of it as a 'physique de l'objet quelconque' (cf. Gonseth's idoneism); but this viewpoint only covers a part of our logico-mathematical knowledge.

(IIa)   For the platonist there is no difficulty. We know 'higher reality' either by immediate intuition, or by induction on the basis of sensory data. This standpoint is irrefutable, but is difficult to reconcile with the general viewpoints which direct science in our time.

(IIb)   The nominalist can make a choice between divergent conceptions. For example, he can join himself to the neo-positivistic doctrine, according to which the question raised here is senseless because the theorems of logic and mathematics are tautologies and therefore express no knowledge.

To support this last doctrine one usually points to (i) the completeness theorem, and (ii) the existence of a decision method. But these arguments are absolutely insufficient. A decision method exists – except for some elementary mathematical theories – only for the sentential calculus; already for the theory of the quantifiers there is no decision method, as Alonzo Church has demonstrated; for the theory of the quantifiers we have the completeness theorems proved by Löwenheim, Skolem, Gödel, Tarski and Henkin, so that if need be we can designate the theorems of the theory of the quantifiers as tautologies. For the theorems of Russell's theory, however, this is, as Ramsey has already remarked, only so if we first cast them in the hypothetical form described in par. 13; for the theorems of Zermelo's theory, even this is no longer true.

The neo-positivistic conception of logic and mathematics is therefore certainly too simplistic. To come to a more correct insight, I make, for the moment, the following distinction between having cognition of and knowing: *cognition* presupposes a transcendental cognitive object, *knowing* does not. We can then say that logic and mathematics according to the intuitionists belongs to knowing, according to the formalist and the platonist rather to cognition. The possibility of a nominalistic interpretation of set theory – and with that of logic and mathematics – indicates, though, that the distinction between knowing and cognition is only relative and perhaps even illusory.

Phenomenologically in my opinion we do best in distinguishing different areas of knowledge (cognition), of which logic and mathematics together form one. The different areas are not completely unrelated, but it is also not possible to reduce one area to the other. We can perhaps characterize their mutual relationship best as *complementary*.

This viewpoint has various important consequences. In the first place it insures the autonomy of the cognitive areas, provided these are not conceived in that dogmatic sense to which I have earlier made objections[20]. The fact that these areas are mutually irreducible can only become clear from the failure of attempts to reduction; in this sense I distinguish cognitive areas of physics, of social life, of self-consciousness, and still others. The complementarity of these areas excludes, except the mutual reducibility, also the subordination of one area to another.

As already said, according to my opinion logic and mathematics together form one autonomous cognitive area. This area derives a completely individual character from the circumstance that on the one hand one obtains knowledge here to which a very high degree of certainty should be ascribed, while on the other hand it turns out to be very difficult to localize a definite cognitive object.

In my opinion the complementarity of this cognitive area with respect to self-consciousness also excludes each more profound and more detailed epistemological clarification. An attempt to do that, for example in the form of a transcendental deduction would have to presuppose that we would fix our attention simultaneously on (i) the knowing subject, (ij) the cognitive object in question, and (iij) the entirety of those relations between knowing subject and cognitive object, by which our knowledge is constituted. And the complementarity now just excludes such a simultaneous consideration of knowing subject and cognitive object.

This does not mean that the logician and mathematician are not in many respects dependent on data of a psychological or physical nature.

But they will make an appeal exclusively to data of a very elementary nature – relating, for example, to the stability of certain memory images or material signs – and they will always arrange it in such a way that they don't have to enter into more complex considerations, so they are rightly little tempted to make the correctness of their conclusions dependent on a cosmological hypothesis as mentioned in par. 11. By way of illustration I mention that much of what is announced as psychology of thinking, in fact has to be counted as logic.

The impossibility of an epistemological clarification concerning the principles of logic and mathematics does not, of course, imply that these principles are not at all suitable for further clarification. But this clarification can only be obtained from logic and mathematics itself. To name an example, we won't obtain a deeper insight about the principle of the excluded third in an introspective way, but perhaps we will by a future development in the area of logic and mathematics.

NOTES

[1] This study has been written under the impression of a summer conference held in Amersfoort, 1953; comp. E. W. Beth [69]. The paragraphs 1–7 are, with some changes, adopted from E. W. Beth [69a].

[2] One should think of the realism of William of Champeaux.

[3] A detailed exposition from a nominalistic standpoint is given by W. V. Quine [2], which also refers to further literature.

[4] E. W. Beth [H], Book v.

[5] It will not be necessary to illustrate this with examples.

[6] Comp. A. Tarski [2], Ch. vi.

[7] It is necessary to point out that such an axiom does not occur with Frege or with Cantor, at least not in this form. I have here, just as in the description of the theories of Russell and Zermelo, proceeded retrospectively in the sense that each time those simplifications have been introduced which have turned out to be possible on the basis of newer – sometimes very recent investigations. Also certain tendencies which I, for the sake of brevity, have mentioned in connection with Frege and Cantor – respectively with Russell and Zermelo, only emerge clearly with later kindred spirits. For further data, comp. E. W. Beth [H] Book iv, chapters 1 and 2.

[8] An excellent – also retrospective – review of the most important axiomatizations in set theory is given in Hao Wang & R. McNaughton [1].

[9] I adopt this suggestive term from Hermes; comp. H. Hermes and H. Scholz [1].

[10] Compare, for example W. V. Quine [2], p. 125.

[11] The phrase *"Al zullen er nog wel wiskundigen zijn, die met Cantor het actueel oneindige en de oneindige verzameling willen aanvaarden..."* ["Although there will still be mathematicians, who, with Cantor, want to accept the actual infinity and the infinite set..."] (P. H. van Laar [1]) could give rise to the impression that Cantor's set theory is no longer applied by the mathematicians of our time. I just want to point out, therefore, that on the contrary its significance increases continuously, and that most of the disciplines characteristic for contemporary mathematics – including certain parts of foundations research – would simply be unimaginable without the basis presented by set theory.

[12] Here we don't have to go into the connection with the nominalism of the Middle Ages, which appears in a new light in E. A. Moody [1].

[13] Thus far this had not come to a clear expression in his writings.

[14] N. Goodman and W. V. Quine [1].

[15] Comp. K. Gödel [2].

[16] I follow here in the main lines the exposition given by Tarski in Amersfoort, but cannot guarantee every detail. Naturally I have taken as much advantage as possible of the data on hand in the available literature.

[17] This definition for the concept of *definability* (in Gödel: *'constructability'*) is given in K. Gödel [1]. The significance of the concept for the problems which occupy us at present is given briefly in K. Gödel [2] and [3]. Comp. also A. Tarski [3].

[18] Comp. E. W. Beth [69] and, on the deduction theorem of Tarski and Herbrand, A. Tarski [2].
[19] Comp. P. Bernays [1] as well as E. W. Beth [H], Slotwoord.
[20] Comp. E. W. Beth [2].

CHAPTER VIII

FORMALIZED LANGUAGE AND COMMON USAGE

1. INTRODUCTION

The objections, raised in connection with the formalization of language, have a very divergent tendency; they direct themselves, among other things, against:

 (i) the construction of formalized languages as such, or certain of its characteristic aspects;

 (ij) the critique on ordinary language, by which the construction of formalized languages is usually motivated;

(iij) the use that is made of formalized languages, for example in mathematical foundational studies;

(iv) the conceptions which are defended concerning the relationship of formalized languages and ordinary language;

 (v) the adoption of aims and directives originating from the study of formalized languages in investigations concerning ordinary language;

(vi) philosophical conclusions based on certain results from the research on formalized language.

It is not my intention to go here into these objections, which are naturally not without any foundation. I prefer to make some remarks about the development inside the research of formalized languages. Such an exposition will of itself obviate a number of objections, while the soundness of others will appear in clearer light.

In the critique on formalization, a clear evolution has taken place in the last decade. Initially the emphasis was on objections, as under (i)–(iij), but this has slowly moved to those under (iv)–(vi). This shift is related to the development, which the research on formalized languages and the mathematical foundational studies went through in the same period.

2. UNIFICATION OF PURE MATHEMATICS

During the last quarter of the 19th century mathematical foundational studies were governed by a powerful trend to the unification of pure mathematics, which found expression both in Frege's logicism and Cantor's set theory.[1] Initially mathematics had occupied itself with objects of a very divergent nature: with *figures* in geometry, with *numbers* in arithmetic, with *variable quantities* and *functions* in analysis. But already Fermat and Descartes had demonstrated in their analytic geometry how one could reduce figures to (real) numbers, and in this direction in the 19th century great progress had been made. Thus, finally, Russell in 1903[2] could state as an accomplished fact the complete unification of pure mathematics:

> ... all pure mathematics deals exclusively with concepts definable in terms of a very small number of fundamental ... concepts, and ... its propositions are deducible from a very small number of fundamental ... principles ...

As is well known Russell goes one step farther:

> ... all mathematics follows from symbolic logic ...,

but I don't yet want to go into this point.

It is better that we concern ourselves first with the question, in which way Russell could justify his first assertion, which just relates to the unification of pure mathematics. The deductive method, peculiar to pure mathematics, leaves only one way open; the following steps are necessary:

(i) listing of the (very few) basic concepts;

(ij) listing of the (very few) basic theorems or axioms [for the sake of brevity I would like to designate these concepts and theorems, which have to present the joint foundation for *all* theories of pure mathematics, as *absolute* basic concepts and as *absolute* basic theorems];

(iij) description of the specific basic concepts of the separate theories of pure mathematics in terms of the absolute basic concepts;

(iv) proof of the specific basic theorems of the separate theories of pure mathematics on the basis of the absolute basic concepts and of the definitions, as described under (iij).

To come to a complete listing of the required absolute basic concepts, as described under (i) and (ij), extremely thorough preparatory analytical studies (for which Frege had already set an example), of which in this connection, however, only the final result matters. The convincing power of the argument stands or falls, however, with the quality of the definitions mentioned under (iij) and the proofs mentioned under (iv). Now the degree of clarity and acuteness which is required here cannot be attained as long as one uses ordinary language in his formulations, as Frege had already seen. One is therefore faced with the choice either to forego the realization of the aim in mind, or go over to the construction of a formalized language. Frege as well as Russell, rather went over to the construction of a formalized language then, to abandon the realization of the goal they had set for themselves.

I imagine that at this point of my argument two questions will be raised:

(i) aren't the objections connected with the usage of ordinary language exaggerated?

(ij) are the definitions and proofs, which the use of a formalized language enabled Frege and Russell to make, indeed faultless?

Who wants to do so can, without too great difficulty, convince himself that the use of ordinary language indeed presents great, yes, even insurmountable difficulties. Both Frege and Russell have published, besides their 'official' exposition, also a more intelligible version.[3] Now Frege, although somewhat dry, is a particularly sharp and clear stylist, and Russell is both brilliant and sharp. In both cases, however, the intelligible version is only intelligible and convincing for those who also are familiar with the formalized versions. With the use of ordinary language all kinds of artificial twists are necessary, the tenor of which only becomes clear by comparison with the official version.

3. THE PARADOXES

In answering the second question we have to take into account the occurrence of the paradoxes, of which the first had been found already in 1895 by Cantor, which were, however, not given much publicity before 1900. In 1903 Russell discovered the paradox which bears his name, which not only unsettled his own still unpublished exposition, but also the one which Frege had published already in 1893. If ever, at that moment the great advantage became clear which can be obtained from the use of a formalized language.

Had Frege and Russell used ordinary language, they could have dismissed the matter with little difficulty. But in a formalized language such a tactic is not available. Once some one has established the 'rules of the game', he has to accept the consequences.

So it turned out to be necessary to subject the formalization and the absolute principles chosen with it to a radical revision. Russell used for that purpose, as is known, the *theory of logical types*. In the years 1910–1913 he published, with Whitehead, *Principia Mathematica,* in which now indeed the program of a unified construction of pure mathematics was realized on a, to all probability, sound foundation.

I now return to Russell's second assertion:

... all mathematics follows from symbolic logic...,

which without doubt also represents Frege's opinion.

This assertion is of great importance because it becomes clear from it that Russell wants to attach a well-defined meaning to the symbols he uses. He is also of the opinion that the axioms presupposed by him should be considered *true,* with which then, of course, at the same time the truth of all theorems of pure mathematics is guaranteed[2]:

The doctrines just mentioned are, in my opinion, quite indispensable to any even tolerably satisfactory philosophy of mathematics, as the following pages will show... the fact that they allow mathematics to be true, which most current philosophies do not, is surely a powerful argument in their favour.

On the basis of these considerations there can be no doubt, however, about the fact that the system of symbols constructed by Russell has to be considered a *language.* Since the meaning of the symbols has been determined (how this happens does not matter at present), the system of symbols can be used to express thoughts. We therefore have to consider this system as a language even if it is a formalized language, the possibilities of expression of which are restricted, with the understanding that, at least according to Russell's intention, it should cover the whole area of formal logic and pure mathematics.

4. HILBERT'S FORMALISM

A completely different situation was created by the rise of Hilbert's formalism, the general tenor of which can be explained without too great difficulties on the basis of the previous sections.

As we have seen, Russell had succeeded in constructing a unified system for formal logic and pure mathematics, whereby such precautionary
measures had been taken as seemed instrumental in the prevention of the
occurrence of new paradoxes.

Russell had not shown, however, that inside his system no paradoxes
could occur any more, and his method hardly opened any horizons in this
direction. Exactly this point, however, had already been taken up in 1900
by Hilbert, who developed in the course of the years a special method to
give consistency proofs.

To understand Hilbert's approach well, we have to return for a moment
to an issue already discussed, in fact the considerations which forced Frege
and Russell to take the paradoxes seriously. We have remarked that the
occurrence of the paradoxes was a result of the 'rules of the game', which
they had presupposed in the construction of the formalized language, i.e.,
of the formal rules for the manipulation of the symbols. The meaning
attached to the symbols does not play any role.

Therefore, to demonstrate that a formalized theory does not contain
a contradiction, we will also have to concentrate our attention on these
formal rules, while we can leave the meaning of the symbols out of
consideration.

This also entails that Hilbert does not consider the formalized language
'from the inside', as a user of the language would, but from the 'outside'.
This is one of the main characteristics of the formalistic standpoint.

For the formalist certain symbols and combinations of symbols are
given, from which, on the basis of certain formal rules (i.e., on the basis of
rules which exclusively refer to the form and order of the symbols, but
not to their meaning), new combinations of symbols can be obtained.
His problem is to prove that the application of these formal rules, however often repeated, will *never* make certain combinations of symbols
appear (namely those which express a contradiction).

I mention still some important consequences of the acceptance of the
formalistic approach. In the first place it appears to be necessary to lay
down the formal rules accurately and completely; it turned out afterwards
that with Russell something was lacking in this respect.

In the second place it will not be advisable to tackle the consistency
proof with regard to a formal system, so all-inclusive as that of the
Principia Mathematica; it's more appropriate to start with systems of a

more restricted nature, and then afterwards to relate more and more inclusive systems to the investigation.

Perhaps even more important is the following. For whoever views a formalized language from the inside, i.e., as a user, a theorem provable within that language is a truth, and therefore worthy of attention in its own right. For the formalist, who views the system from the outside, and foregoes the meaning of the symbols, a separate theorem is of little importance; the formalist is interested in the first place in the formal system as a whole.

5. SOME INVESTIGATIONS OF GÖDEL AND TARSKI

The principle motive for Hilbert to forego the meaning of the symbols which occur in a formal system was cited among the difficulties which arise when we try to establish this meaning with the same degree of accuracy we practised in the statement of the formal rules.

This difficulty, however, is not insurmountable. There is a simple way out, as especially Gödel has demonstrated, for those formal systems which arise in the formalization of arithmetic or of some part thereof. In such a system combinations of symbols would occur which initially were intended as a notation for natural numbers. In the formal rules this finds no direct expression. Nevertheless it sometimes appears already from the structure of certain combinations of symbols, for example:

IIIII

that they would be suitable as notations for certain natural numbers. And likewise it can already appear from the structure of certain formulas, for example:

[III, II] // IIIII

that they would be suitable as formulations of certain arithmetical truths. We can now make use of the established connection between symbols and formulas, on the one hand, and natural numbers and arithmetical truths on the other hand (a connection, the establishment of which is based only on the formal rules), without having to abandon the formal standpoint.

Tarski's semantics allows us to obtain a corresponding result, also for systems of non-arithmetical origin.

If we now make use of these observations, then we come to some very

surprising conclusions. It turns out that the metamathematical consideration of a formal system in its entirety has a much more complicated
mathematical content than Hilbert had foreseen.

This is expressed in the famous results of Gödel and Tarski, of which
the general idea, to the extent that it matters at present, can be clarified as
follows. It is conceivable that in a formalization F of a part of arithmetic
all theorems:

$$1 + 1 = 1 + 1, 1 + 2 = 2 + 1, 2 + 1 = 1 + 2, 1 + 3$$
$$= 3 + 1, 2 + 2 = 2 + 2, 3 + 1 = 1 + 3, 1 + 4 = 4 + 1, \ldots$$
ad inf.

are provable, while the general theorem:

(1) *for all x and y*: $x + y = y + x,$

is not provable (this is, in principle, a variant on the antique paradox of
the *sorites*). In a metamathematical theory *MF* which allows us to view
the system F as one whole, it will then be provable:

(2) *for each m and n the theorem* $m + n = n + m$ *is provable in F,*

and this theorem can in *MF* serve as a substitute for theorem (1), in case it
might not be provable in F.

6. THE TREATMENT OF FORMAL SYSTEMS AND FORMALIZED LANGUAGES IN LOGICAL AND MATHEMATICAL FOUNDATIONS RESEARCH

The development briefly characterized here, during the years 1903–1931,
which in the meantime has again been followed by an equally long period
of adjustment and consolidation, has determined the manner in which
one deals with formalized languages at present.

It is actually better to distinguish the concept *formal system* from the
concept *formalized language,* in the sense that the first is taken as genus
and the second as species. We can then speak of a formal system as soon
as some precisely described formal rules, in the sense discussed before,
have been given. Such a formalized system only becomes a formalized
language as, moreover, for the symbols of the system a well-determined
meaning has been established in a suitable way. As a rule it does not
matter whether the establishment of the meaning occurs with the greatest

possible precision. Indeed, who has understood the meaning of the symbols can use the formal system as a *language*, to express and communicate his thoughts; if he wants to *prove* the correctness of his thoughts within this language, he will, of course, have to take heed of the formal rules.

(I) We now consider in the first place the case, that one wants to set up and develop a certain deductive theory in a very accurate manner. The obvious means for that purpose is the construction of a formal system, which can serve as a means of expression for a theory in question. The formal rules can now be described exactly so that there never has to be a doubt as to the question whether a given proof has been conducted correctly. As, however, in the construction of the system, the thought of one well-determined interpretation of the symbols is a guiding influence, we have to speak in this case of a formalized language.

This situation mainly occurs in the development of fragments of logic and arithmetic, where one sometimes is anxious not to use certain principles. In the case of logic, it occurs that one does not want to make an appeal to the principle of the excluded third, in arithmetic one sometimes avoids the application of the principle of complete induction. If one uses a formal system, then one is protected from a veiled appeal to these principles.

Another example is presented by the different formalizations of set theory, which have the intention of preventing one from making an appeal to principles, which can give rise to the occurrence of paradoxes.

(II) Now there can be circumstances which make it desirable that to certain symbols a non-standard interpretation is attached, or at least that one foregoes the interpretation originally attached to certain symbols. Such a situation especially arises if one wants to deal with the question, what happens if one omits certain axioms or replaces them by others. In such a case the formal system will lose the property of formalized language.

Nevertheless such experiments are always intended to deepen the insight into the structure of the initially constructed formalized language. So the case discussed under (I) always keeps its fundamental character, and we will confine ourselves mainly to this case.

7. FORMALIZED LANGUAGES AND COMMON USAGE

In a case as meant under (I), it can happen that really all proofs are conducted within the formalized language. This method, however, presents in practice various difficulties.

 (i) In a formalized argumentation one cannot omit a single step. One must therefore put up with very long reasonings of an extremely elementary character, which detract the attention from the essentials.

 (ii) The drawing up of a formalized proof requires much care, and especially much time, and the work spent on the formulation of a long argument of an elementary character is usually not very worthwhile.

(iii) Formalized proofs are difficult to read. Conventional abbreviation of elementary arguments generally makes reading still more difficult.

(iv) Formalized proofs entail high printing costs and are therefore difficult to publish.

On the basis of these, and similar practical considerations, one usually prefers only to formalize the critical phases of the argument. Such a critical phase, as in the cases earlier mentioned as examples, can be caused by the evasion of the seemingly inevitable appeal to the principle of the excluded third or the principle of complete induction. On the basis of over a century's experience, we, of course, know where the critical points lie.

One presents the more elementary parts of the argument by means of ordinary language. Thus one uses a curious style, in which the sentence structure is adapted as much as possible to the structure of the logical formulas which one omits.

I want to mention a characteristic example of this. The equivalence of two conditions C and C' can be expressed by the logical formula:

$$C = C'$$

(one usually uses a symbol different from the equality sign, but this does not matter). The standard formulation in French is:

Pour que C, il faut et il suffit que C'.

During the last years, though, the following formulation has emerged:

C, si et seulement si C'.

I can only explain this by the desire to let the formulation in ordinary language correspond as much as possible to the structure of the logical formula. If the new formulation will be able to supplant the old one, in the long run, remains to be seen. If, however, it takes root in scientific literature, then its inclusion, in common usage via mathematics instruction, is just a question of time. Closer investigation could probably reveal more examples of the influence of formalized languages on daily usage. By the way, traditional logic has also, without doubt, left its traces in ordinary language.

About the influencing of formalized language by common usage nothing needs really to be said. It is clear that in the construction of formalized languages even if there is there an extensive usage of conventional symbols, many elements are derived from common usage. A fascinating problem in this connection is the relationship of the current formalized languages to, say, Chinese or Japanese. As far as I know, however, no exact data are available on this matter.

I have to dedicate in this connection some words to the critique of common usage which often has to serve as motivation for the construction and use of formalized languages. In judgement of this critique one should not lose sight of the fact that formalized languages practically exclusively have to serve as means of expression for deductive theories, while common usage is mainly used for completely different purposes. One cannot expect that common usage completely satisfies all requirements for a means of expression of a deductive theory, and one therefore should not take exception to a discussion about its shortcomings in this regard; such discussions are necessary, because they imply directives for the construction of suitable formalized languages.

8. THE INVESTIGATION OF FORMALIZED LANGUAGES AND LINGUISTICS

In the investigation of formalized languages (logic), the leading viewpoint is its application as means of expression for deductive theories; this viewpoint, in the investigation of common usage is, of course, of only minor importance.

Nevertheless modern logic apparently has a certain influence on linguistics. In this connection we should make a distinction between two main areas of logic, namely:

(i) *syntax*, which exclusively pertains to the structure and order of the symbols, and which therefore can also be characterized as a theory of formal systems; and:

(ii) *semantics*, which mainly investigates the meaning of symbols and combinations of symbols. Within semantics one can, with Quine,[5] make a distinction between a *theory of meaning* and a *theory of reference*, but the point is not taken into consideration here.

Logical syntax has, of course, its linguistic counterpart, but we cannot expect linguistical syntax to work as "formalistically" as logical syntax. Related to logical syntax is, it appears to me, L. Hjelmslev's *glossematics*,[6] which, by the way, seems to have been strongly influenced by ideas from contemporary logic. I cannot judge the value of this direction in linguistics.

Semantics places us in a very complicated situation. For here logic cannot back out of extending its investigations also to common usage. Because the significance of the symbols of a formalized language can only be clarified by means of common usage, logic enters an area here in which not only linguistics, but also general philosophy is traditionally interested. The problem of *analytic judgements* (or *propositions*), for example, can be approached equally from the direction of logic, linguistics or philosophy.

I would like to add to Nuchelmans' discussion of this problem[11] the following considerations, not to dispute his conclusions, but to shed light on the situation from another angle. I cite for this purpose two short fragments of a Platonic dialogue which recently were brought to light.

I

Socrates. Mother, are bachelors always unmarried?
Mother. Yes, son.
S. Aren't bachelors allowed to marry then, Mother?
M. Certainly they are, son, but if they are married, they are no longer bachelors.
S. Why not, Mother?
M. That's written in the laws, son, because they would otherwise have to pay too much taxes. But now you must stop asking questions, because I must attend to a confinement.
Socrates. Father, are priest always married?
Father. Yes, son.
S. Aren't priests allowed to marry then, father?
F. Certainly they are, son, but if they are married they are no longer priests.
S. Why not, father? Is that perhaps a law?

F.   Oh, no, son, how do you get that idea? It just as with a General in the Army. If he was transferred to the Navy, he would no longer be a General, but an Admiral. In the same manner a married priest is no longer called a priest, but a pastor.

These conversations, I believe, illustrate rather nicely the observation made by Nuchelmans that, as a rule, one has a didactic intention, when one pronounces an analytic judgement. This observation is, it appears to me, very correct, but incomplete in two respects.

In the first place the observation does not only hold for analytic, but just as much for all general judgements. In the second place there is, besides the didactical, still another completely different context which in a natural way leads to the pronouncement of general and in particular analytical judgements, namely the exposition of a deductive theory. And now I believe that the advocates of the conception contested by Nuchelmans, only have in mind a context of the second type, and that with regard to this second type their conception is acceptable.

I deem this question of importance because it demonstrates that common usage also, if it is used as a means of expression for a deductive theory, to a certain extent assumes the character of a formalized language.

9. ORDINARY LANGUAGE AS A MEANS OF EXPRESSION FOR DEDUCTIVE THEORIES

In the previous sections we have enlarged on the shortcomings of common usage as a means of expression for deductive theories. This does not alter the fact that since Euclid, common usage has been used for this purpose on a grand scale, a practice which, as it looks now, will be continued for a very long time. A certain justification of this practice is already implied in the considerations of paragraph 7. The degree of precision which can only be attained by using a formalized language need not always be pursued, while the use of a formalized language entails all kinds of practical objections. On the other hand one can render the shortcomings of common usage for a great part harmless, by taking precautionary measures, among which I mention:

(i) the use of a very restricted vocabulary;

(ij) the use of simple sentence constructions, standardized in as much as possible;

(iij) avoiding figurative usage.

On the basis of experience acquired in the construction and use of formalized languages, one knows rather accurately where the pitfalls lie.

In using common usage one even has the opportunity to omit some exactitudes which do not matter; I illustrate this with a simple example. Let us imagine we are formalizing geometry where the concept *parallel* is represented by the well known symbol $//$. We will then obtain the following (axioms or) theorems:

(1) $(l)\,(m)\,[l\,//\,m \to m\,//\,l]$,
(2) $(l)\,(m)\,(n)\,[(l\,//\,m\;\&\;m\,//\,n) \to l\,//\,n]$,

and each appeal to one of these theorems will have to be mentioned *in extenso* (this is the practical difficulty mentioned in the beginning of par. 7 under (i)). If we want to obtain a high degree of precision while using common usage, then we can represent $l//m$ as: *l is parallel to m*, and we thus obtain:

(1′) *for each l and m: if l is parallel to m, them n is parallel to l,*

(2′) *for each l, m and n: if l is parallel to m, and m parallel to n, then l is parallel to n,*
which does not essentially give an abbreviation, but is easier to read. Now if we want, for the sake of an essential abbreviation, to put up with a lower degree of accuracy, then we represent $l//m$ as: *l and m are parallel*, through which the 'translation' of (1) and (2) starts sounding so 'tautological', that the need for mentioning an application of these theorems will hardly be felt. So this way of formulating is the most concise.

[Actually we give here common usage too much honor. We can, if we formalize geometry, prove the following *metatheorem*:

> Let $C\,(l)$ be a condition formulated exclusively in terms of $//$, and let $C\,(m)$ be the condition, which is created by replacing l by m; then:
> $(l)\,(m)\,[l\,//\,m \to \{C\,(l) \to C\,(m)\}]$,
> is a theorem. –

This metatheorem includes, in a manner of speaking, an infinite supply of geometric theorems, and its application results in considerable abbreviations.]

We now imagine that we want to construct a *deductive theory of the census bureau* CB, using ordinary language. In this theory there will occur concepts like *man, woman, married, husband, marriageable, of age, bachelor.* In CB, among other things one will assert:

(1)   *All bachelors are unmarried.*

What now is the status of this proposition? The answer to this question will depend on the manner in which we construct CB. In the first place it is possible that proposition (1) is chosen as an axiom. It is also conceivable that (1) can be derived from the axioms in a very complicated way.

The most obvious thing, however, is to introduce it as a definition:

(2)   *A bachelor is an unmarried marriageable man,*

and in this case (1) assumes the character of an (applied) 'tautology'.

With this, however (in that I completely agree with Nuchelmans) the problem of Socrates is *not* solved. From the standpoint taken here, one cannot make any distinction between the problems stated in dialogues I and II. We can, for example, very well set up a *deductive theory of the clerical census bureau,* CCB, in which the definitions:

(1)   *A priest is an unmarried clergyman,*
(2)   *A pastor is a married clergyman,*

are assumed, so that we can prove in CCB the following theorems:

(3)   *All priests are unmarried,*
(4)   *All pastors are married.*

We encounter here the distinction made already by Kant[7] between *analytic* and *synthetic* usage. In analytic usage we have to take the words in their current meaning; in synthetic usage, on the other hand, the meaning of the words is established by means of axioms, definitions and such. Whether we are dealing with analytic or synthetic usage is dependent on the intentions of the speaker. These intentions are sometimes expressly stated and in other cases can be deduced from the general drift of his argument.

I would have liked to make from this point of view some remarks on the contributions of Wiersma[8], Vredenduin[9] and Ubbink[10], but this would take me too far at present.

10. 'SYNTHETIC' AND 'NORMAL' USAGE

To avoid misunderstandings, however, I have to point out that *synthetic* usage does not coincide with what Nuchelmans designates as *normal* usage.[11]

A synthetic definition has a normative tenor: the defined term ought to be conceived and used within the theory in question in this and no other way. An analytic definition describes the normal usage of a term; it does not exclude a deviating usage, it just stamps this to a usage in a 'metaphorical or modified sense'; moreover it facilitates the explanation of deviating usage, because it connects it with normal usage.

It happens that the meaning of a term described in a synthetic definition deviates considerably from the normal usage (the term '*work*' in physics presents a well known example), but usually this is not so. In most cases the synthetic definition aims mainly at preventing usage of a term in a 'metaphorical or modified sense', and in that case, the synthetic and analytic definitions could coincide *de facto*.

There are also, however, many examples of terms (one thinks of '*volt*' and '*atomic nucleus*', or of the French expression '*en fonction de*'), which initially made their entry into scientific language on the basis of synthetic definitions, and then afterwards, with no significant change of meaning, were also adopted into common usage. The picture is further complicated because synthetic definitions are drawn up sometimes incidentally, as if in passing, in a connection where one doesn't expect them, and nevertheless gain influence over ordinary language (for example 'earth satellite', a term which would have been inadmissible for Ptolemy).

This development to a certain extent, gives to common usage the character, by nature foreign to it, of a formalized language; this gives the results obtained in the study of formalized languages a certain relevance for general linguistics. One can regret this development, but he will have a hard time stopping it, and he will not be able to leave it out of consideration without violating the intention of a certain group of language users.[12]

NOTES

[1] E. W. Beth [89] comp. p. 92.
[2] B. Russell [1]; more detailed quotations with comments in E. W. Beth [H], pp. 199–200. – In this last work (esp. pp. 86–92, 104–108, 160–163, 198–206, 244–246,

300–301) one also finds some basic considerations about the subject of this study. One also finds more data about the investigations of Gödel and Tarski, and about the work of Th. Skolem, which is somewhat older.

[3] G. Frege [1], B. Russell [2].
[4] Comp. however about Chinese M. Masterman [1].
[5] W. V. Quine [2].
[6] Comp. B. Siertsema [1].
[7] E. W. Beth [74].
[8] H. A. Weersma [1]; comp. H. Scholz [1].
[9] P. G. J. Vredenduin [1].
[10] J. B. Ubbink [1].
[11] G. Nuchelmans [1].
[12] B. Russell [3].

CHAPTER IX

CONSIDERATIONS ABOUT LOGICAL THOUGHT

The considerations about logical thought, which I may hereby put before you, are partly to be taken as an after thought on my rather recent work about *The Foundations of Mathematics*[1], but they partly also anticipate two works which are still in preparation.* I may therefore forego detailed documentation.

A philosophical consideration about the nature of logical thought and about the foundations of logic cannot exclusively rest on an analysis of the conceptions which are characteristic of contemporary logic, but also should take into account conceptions of the past. Even if such conceptions have been completely superseded by later investigations, still the mere fact that they were once current can give us material for fruitful speculations.

We can, roughly taken, distinguish in the conceptions about logic three phases: (i) the *traditional phase*, (ij) the *psychologizing phase*, and (iij) the *mathematizing phase*. The traditional phase I let begin with Aristotle, of course, the psychologizing with Descartes and Locke, and the mathematizing with Boole and De Morgan. Sharp boundaries are of course impossible to draw, either in chronological or doxographical respects. Tradition just happens to have needed many centuries to establish itself, psychology after Descartes has gone through many transformations. Mathematics, too, is in no way unalterably given: a development in abstract direction has brought it closer to logic. Finally: both the psychologizing and the mathematizing logic can, with a certain right, invoke Aristotle.

Nevertheless each of the phases mentioned shows a physiognomy of its own, and a relatively very strong and conscious continuity. At the same time the mathematizing phase signifies in various regards a return (by no means always intended) to traditional conceptions as a reaction to psychologism.

Meanwhile by the way, this has not kept the proponents of traditional and psychologizing logic from forming over a long time a closed front against mathematizing tendencies. What will have discouraged many of them was probably, mainly, the extent and complexity of mathematical logic and its (often proclaimed with too much emphasis) conventional and artificial character. In judging such objections, one should meanwhile take into account the influence of trivializing tendencies in the development of logic.

A trivializing tendency is almost by nature inherent in the practice of logic. Who is convinced of the fundamental significance of logic for science and for human thought in general will tend to facilitate the study of logic as much as possible; he will also be inclined to announce the subject of this study as a very elementary business; as an illustration of the effectiveness of this tendency, also in modern mathematical logic, I refer to L. Wittgenstein's characterization of the logical laws as '*tautologies*' [2], to K. R. Popper's studies about *The Trivialization of Mathematical Logic* [3], to W. V. Quine's *Methods of Logic*, [4] and to my own communication about *Semantic Entailment and Formal Derivability*. [5] You will not expect me to disapprove of such tendencies; to the contrary, my opinion remains that rigorous concentration on the essential and elementary is conducive to philosophical insight.

However, one can also go too far in this direction. That already the traditional phase has gone very far in this direction is apparent from the well known rhymes and mnemonic devices, many of which can be found collected in I. M. Bocheński's *Formale Logik*. [6] That it has gone too far will be apparent from the fact that the fundamental logical literature of Greek antiquity has been transmitted to us, with few exceptions, only fragmentarily, and that part of what remained preserved was no longer understood any more in the long run, and consequently came to be reputed as useless subtlety and sterile hairsplitting.

This hollowing out of the logical tradition took at long last *such* forms that the little which remained current could indeed, with some right, be called sterile and useless. This explains as well the deep contempt for these remainders which finds expression in Ramus and Descartes in the endeavor for a new construction which ushers in the psychologizing phase.

Psychologizing logic accepted in the first instance the heritage of traditional logic but saw itself in its way compelled to continue with the trivialization. As the anonymous writers of the *Logique de Port-Royal* argue in their *Avis*[7], this work, famed for centuries, was written to demonstrate that somebody with a good aptitude would not need more than four or five days to learn as much logic as could be useful. That Locke still recognized the existence of abstract ideas was recognized by Berkeley as an inconsistency: abstracta have no psychical reality. That in mathematics one reasons logically is according to Descartes and Kant an illusion. And finally K. Marbe argued in his *Experimentell-psychologische Untersuchungen über das Urteil* [8]:

> Wenn wir nun noch einmal auf unsere psychologischen Untersuchungen des Urteils zurückblicken, so dürfen wir wohl ohne weiteres behaupten, dass, wie weit jene Untersuchungen auch fortgesetzt werden mögen, sie niemals geeignet sein werden, die logischen Probleme direkt zu fördern. ... Die Logik, die gegenwärtig in vielen Stücken nichts anderes als eine unmethodische Psychologie des Urteils ist, wird sich daher künftig so unpsychologisch als möglich zu gestalten haben.

With that trivialization had definitively reached the absolute zero, and at the same time the psychologizing tendency in logic had signed its own death warrant.

I would not like to be misunderstood at this point of my argument. I know that objections can be raised against Marbe's experiments and that the 'Würzburger Schule' hasn't stood still at this conclusions. But this does not affect the soundness of Marbe's experimental results in the context of my argument. An attempt to base a logical theory on introspective or experimental-psychological data makes sense only when an extremely elementary and unambiguous character can be ascribed to these data.

On the other hand the rejection of the psychological foundation of logic in no way necessitates a denial of the right to existence of a *thought psychology* as it has been developed notably by the 'Würzburger Schule'. Such a thought psychology will hardly be able to contribute anything to the handling of the problems of the foundations of logic, which are connected with the repeated emergence of *paradoxes* or *antimonies*; although it will make the very divergent reactions to these problems somewhat more understandable.

It is true, as I have already indicated, that the psychologizing phase had set in as a reaction to the fact that trivializing tendencies within traditional logic were gaining more and more ground, tendencies which had led to the elimination of all sorts of things which were not understood any more and which were therefore stigmatized as fruitless subtleties and useless hairsplitting, but it saw itself soon compelled to continue the trivialization in its own way. The circumstance that finally only a very concise and strongly simplified extract from antique and medieval logic remained current explains that the proponents of traditional as well as of psychological logic initially showed little understanding and even less appreciation for the rise of mathematical logic. Mathematical logic, on the other hand, has thrown a completely new light on many subtleties from the older logic which were no longer understood.

In my *Foundations*[9] I have analyzed three of the so-called sophisms of Eubulides of Milete: each of these apparently could be seen as an objection against a tenet defended by Aristotle. This interpretation finds support in the circumstance that the opposition to Aristotle by Eubulides – be it without reference to the sophisms – is mentioned expressly by other sources, and that, moreover, Aristotle's response to the objections has been handed down to us. As a rounding off and confirmation of my interpretation I would now like to discuss Eubulides' *cornutus*; this sophism can be worded as follows:

Opponens: Have you ever lost horns?
Defendens: No, I have never lost horns.
Opponens: What you have not lost, that you have got; but you have lost no horns; therefore you have horns.

The wording of the argument could easily tempt us not to take it seriously. But that would certainly be wrong: also in the contemporary literature of philosophy of science humoristically worded arguments often occur, (in both cases, also very possibly a trivializing tendency expresses itself here). Moreover Aristotle's reaction proves that he himself took the argument very seriously.

We now denote what Defendens has not lost as *A*, what he possesses as *B*, and the Defendens' horns as *C*. The reasoning of Opponens then takes the following form:

$$\begin{array}{l} \text{All } A\text{'s are } B \\ \underline{\text{All } C\text{'s are } A} \\ \therefore \text{Some } C\text{'s are } B \end{array}$$

This is a syllogism in the so-called *subaltern modus* BARBARI; it is true that this syllogism was only explicitly dealt with in the Middle Ages, but its soundness cannot be doubted on the basis of the principles of Aristotle's syllogistics. On the other hand, the reasoning of Opponens is clearly not acceptable for natural thought. We may therefore conclude that on the basis of the principles of Aristotle's syllogistics, we have to grant validity to reasonings which are not acceptable for natural thought.

In the first instance Eubulides' *cornutus* apparently is directed against the principles of Aristotle's syllogistics; that he would want to contest these is also plausible on other grounds. From Aristotle's response it seems to follow that Eubulides has not stopped at this point, but has also related the *method of exposition* to his polemic; critical considerations about this method in Alexander Aphrodisias, briefly indicated in my *Foundations*, could therefore originate with Eubulides' polemic. And finally Aristotle's response suggests a connection with the famous antinomy of the *Third Man*, which I have also discussed briefly in my *Foundations*. All this, by the way, would be obvious from the standpoint of the extreme realism that Eubulides, as spokesman of the Megaric School, must have defended. However, I will not go more deeply into these points at present.

Now with regard to Aristotle's syllogistics, the question here is the granting of '*existential import*' to universal propositions, which implies the exclusion of 'empty' terms (such as in our case the term C, or 'Defendens' horns'). The *Quaestio, utrum haec sit vera: homo est animal, nullo homine existente*, of Siger van Brabant, clearly relates to this point. That it does not concern superfluous hairsplittings is apparent from the fact that this question came up for discussion again in the development of mathematical logic. Its proponents are in the vast majority prepared to allow 'empty' terms; so they do not grant '*existential import*' to universal propositions and therefore reject a number of traditionally recognized modi of the syllogisms, along with others the modus BARBARI.

P. F. Strawson, one of the leading figures of the English Analytic School (which does not, like the American, continue the tradition of logical empiricism, but, rather, joins up with the later work of Wittgenstein), wants to grant 'existential import' to universal propositions, and so agrees in this regard with Aristotle. He does not appeal, however, to the rejection of 'empty' terms, but to a rule of common usage according to which the *use* '*presupposes*' that the term is not 'empty', without thereby affirming this presupposition (even implicitly).

This last addition is necessary because 'presupposing' in this connection has to be understood as 'presupposing *until further notice*'. The universal proposition: 'all witches are dangerous' presupposes the existence of witches without, however, affirming this existence. We can therefore follow up with: 'but witches don't exist', without having to take the first proposition back because of that; we have thus merely dropped this presupposition.

If one wants to defend Aristotle's syllogistics, as Strawson aims to do in his *Introduction to Logical Theory*[10], then one should extend the '*existential import*' somewhat farther still. I would therefore like to formulate the rule of common usage to which Strawson appeals as follows: the use of a term presupposes an '*existential import*' without, however, affirming it for the time being; if, however, this presupposition is not dropped in time, then it is tacitly confirmed.

May the *cornutus* serve as an illustration. The Opponens uses the terms 'horns' (i.e. 'of Defendens') and therefore presupposes its existential import, without, for the time being affirming it. Defendens therefore still has the opportunity of discarding the '*existential import*', for example by posing the counter-question: 'What horns do you mean?' He misses this opportunity, however, so that now the '*existential import*' is assumed to be affirmed, and the Opponens makes grateful use of this.

From this it is again evident that the full purport of a proposition in ordinary language can only be judged in a wider connection. The English Analytic School stresses strongly, for that reason, the importance of context, and it even reproaches the students of mathematical logic for having too little feel for this curious aspect of common usage.

A more unreasonable reproach is hardly imaginable; it moreover arises from neglecting the context. Since Aristotle logic has used the *analytical method* recommended by him: each proof is decomposed into syllogisms, each syllogism into propositions (premises and conclusion), each proposition into terms. The consistent application of this method apparently requires that we disengage the syllogisms, propositions, and terms from the wider context in which they occur; this necessarily entails that we dispense with the peculiarity of common usage pointed out by Strawson and his supporters, which, by the way, makes it in its normal usage an unsuitable means of expression for logical reasoning.

If one nevertheless wants to use common usage as a means of expression and especially if one nevertheless wants to apply the analytical method to the investigation of reasonings formulated in ordinary language, then one therefore has to insure that, no matter what the intent of each syllogism, each proposition and term can be determined without considering a wider context. One therefore should establish this intent unambiguously once and for all, and thus perforce lapses into artifices which naturally always mean an infraction on the rules valid for the normal usage. In particular we will have to dispense in some way or another with rules of usage such as the one Strawson appeals to.

In Aristotle we find one possible solution to this problem: he excludes 'empty' terms and therefore grants once and for all '*existential import*' to each universal proposition. Traditional syllogistics consistently is based on this principle. That it entails an infringement upon the rules of normal usage is evident from our analysis of Eubulides' *cornutus*. On the other hand it is in accordance with the practice of Greek science, which only admits the introduction of new terms by definition if at the same time a proof is presented of the existence of objects to which these terms apply: a well-known example is given by Proposition I in Book I of Euclides' *Elements*, which serves to justify the definition of the term 'equilateral triangle.'

One can raise various objections to Aristotle's solution.

(i) The exclusion of 'empty' terms and the requirement or *real* thereby implied, and not only *nominal* definitions are valid for the *apodictic* argumentations and not for the *dialectic*. The doctrine of syllogism, strictly speaking, as by the way was Aristotle's intention, holds for the former and not the latter; a *general* theory of reasoning is not given by it.

(ij) Complications can arise in the judgment of proofs by contradiction. It can occur that a term is designated as non-'empty' on the basis of a supposition which we want to take *ad absurdum*. This then justifies the application of certain syllogisms which finally produce the desired contradiction. The introduced assumption has now been refuted, and it *then* becomes evident that the term in question is 'empty'. But by this the foundation for the applied syllogisms seems to be nullified; thus doubt can arise as to the soundness of the conclusion.

(iij) By far the most serious objection against Aristotle's solution lies, however, in the fact that it entails an infraction on the *formal character* of logic; for in many cases the answer to the question whether a certain term is 'empty' or not is dependent on empirical data. Eubulides *cornutus* can again serve as illustration. On the basis of Aristotle's syllogistics the soundness of this argument can only be contested on the basis of the fact that the term 'horns of Defendens' is 'empty'; and we can only know this on the basis of empirical data.

With the acceptance of Aristotle's solution the distinction between the *formal* question as to the *soundness* of a given reasoning and the *material* question as to the *truth* or *falsity* of its premises and conclusion is abrogated; with this distinction, however, the whole right to existence of formal logic as such is invalidated.

Although strictly speaking this objection is not valid in the area of mathematics, in practice one has even here long since abandoned the questionable principle of Aristotle's logistics. One calmy introduces terms by means of nominal definitions, thereby not excluding 'empty' terms, and therefore does not grant *'existential import'* to universal propositions as such. One cannot therefore in the least blame mathematical logic for infringing on the rules of common usage, for example in the sense that it does not grant *'existential import'* to universal propositions. In the first place such a reproach is unreasonable because scientific usage simply is not normal usage, and in the second place because mathematical logic usually replaces common usage with all kinds of *formalized languages* which are more suitable to its purposes. Furthermore, as we have seen, the use of common usage as a means of expression for logical reasoning will always entail an infraction on the normal rules of usage. Aristotle could not avoid such an infraction, either, even though he did not go as far in this respect as contemporary logicians. That mathematical logic goes farther finds a justification not merely in considerations derived from contemporary practice of science, but especially in the demands which result from the formal character of logic; the conventional and artificial elements in mathematical logic are of much less importance than is often assumed.

Let us join to this brief historic resume a short discussion of a more anthropological nature. The historical facts seem to demonstrate that man, under certain circumstances, and to a certain extent, possesses both the tendency and the ability to what one designates as *logical thinking*. This logical thinking manifests itself in the first instance in concrete reasonings as we can encounter them, notably in philosophy and mathematics. In a certain sense we can designate as a higher manifestation the general logical theory of which Aristotle's syllogistics forms the oldest known example.

Although logical thinking lends itself to many-faceted applications, its value cannot be determined by external standards, because it is not completely contained in any of its applications. Its value can only be judged on the basis of norms which are either already produced by logical thinking itself, or are inherent in logical thinking as such.

As every manifestation of human mental activity, logical thinking, too, looks for a suitable medium. In the first instance it chooses for that purpose, of course, common usage; but if common usage, in spite of more or less violent attempts to adapt it, falls short of expectations, then logical thinking takes recourse in the construction of formalized languages which enables a more adequate means of expression.

One will perhaps be inclined not to rate too highly the readiness and the ability of man for logical thinking. On the other hand the passionate debates which logical problems time and again elicit, indicate that logical thinking forms an essential attribute of human nature. Even those who expect exclusively or mainly anthropological reflection of philosophy, will therefore not be able to deny logic a certain measure of philosophical interest.

Doubtlessly philosophy has in the past directed its attention, to its detriment, often too exclusively to the rationality of man. By lack of philosophical interest, logic, meanwhile, runs into the serious danger of alienating its spiritual origin and of degenerating into a pure technique.

A philosophical study of logic, as I want to advocate here, will never possess a specialistic character. It requires, to the contrary, a broad base and various lines of approach. I would personally like to call attention to the following points:

(1) the foundations and systematic construction of logic;
(2) common usage as a medium of logical thinking;
(3) the psychological investigation of logical thinking;
(4) the history of logic;
(5) the logic of non-Western cultures.

On each of these points I would like to make a small number of brief observations.

(1) The mathematizing phase has to a particular extent deepened our insights into the *foundations* and the *systematic construction of logic*. It has not, as is sometimes alleged, come forth from a misdirected ambition to apply mathematical methods in the treatment of logical problems; rather it is characterized by the analysis of the logical elements which are partly explicitly, partly implicitly present in mathematics. In my opinion it cannot be doubted that these elements are nowhere so plentiful and so easily accessible as in mathematics; moreover in by far the most cases one judges the admissibility of a given definition or proof in mathematics unanimously, what in other areas is generally not the case. The opinion that logical reasoning is not governed by the general principles of logic finds no support in the facts, at least in classical (non-intuitionistic) mathematics.

It is true that it is not always easy to draw the boundary between logic on the one hand and pure (formal or abstract) mathematics on the other; the independent character of logic is apparent, however, from the circumstance that its practice gives rise to the statement of all kinds of problems which would not easily come up in a mathematician. I have given much attention to this kind of problem in the last years; in the long run the results of investigations in this direction will doubtlessly find application both in mathematics and elsewhere. [What regards the first I may now refer to the recent articles of S. Feferman and R. L. Vaught[11] and of R. C. Lyndon.[12]]

It sounds perhaps paradoxical when I say that modern mathematical foundational studies have created the possibility for the construction of formal logic as an independent science. I mention therefore, as a precedent, the close connection which exists in Aristotle between the construction of logic and mathematical foundational studies.

Still Le Blond, *Logique et méthode chez Aristote*[13], denies the existence of a close and essential connection on this point. He appeals, however, to Brunschvicg, Hamelin, and Milhaud, and the ideas of these writers have been strongly influenced by the doctrine of Descartes, who, as I have already observed, is of the opinion that in mathematics one does not reason logically at all. The absurdity of Le Blond's standpoint is apparent from a curious book by H. G. Apostle, *Aristotle's Philosophy of Mathematics*[14], in which the remarks on the foundations of mathematics which occur, scattered through Aristotle, have been joined together, practically without the aid of connecting text, to a surprisingly good running argument that fills more than 200 pages in print.

(2) As I have explained, common usage as a medium for *logical thinking* falls short more or less seriously in various regards. Nevertheless, logical thinking still makes extensive use of this medium. The investigation of what one calls the *logic of common usage* is in fact meaningful and can, as may have become clear from the discussion of an idea of Strawson, contribute to the clarification of insight.

I doubt however whether such an investigation will be able to lead to results which, as the analytical school appears to intend, would possess a normative meaning for general logic. The logician who employs common usage takes a number of precautions in order to obviate certain annoying peculiarities of this medium. In an extreme case he would not stop short of making an infraction on the normal rules of usage. Mostly, however, he would be able to confine himself to avoiding the use of certain 'dangerous' words and phrases, and to employ as much as possible a more or less standardized word choice and sentence construction. This tendency stands out clearly in traditional logic.

(3) Even though logic has outgrown the psychologizing phase, there still remains room, of course, for a *psychological investigation of logical thinking* as a branch of thought psychology. Formerly I occupied myself with problems in this area, and I therefore look forward to the opportunity offered to me by an experienced investigator as Jean Piaget to take up its study again in collaboration with him.

I insert here the following remark, although the connection with the previous observations will not be immediately clear. In my communication on *Semantic Entailment and Formal Derivability*, I referred to the possible construction of a '*logical machine*' which would be able to execute the logical deductions described by me. At that time I did not think of practical applications. Since then, however, the following developments took place.

(i) Deduction methods related to the ones proposed by me can also be found in independent publications of K. J. J. Hintikka (1955), K. Schütte (1956) and S. Kanger (1957)[15] and also in the (unpublished) dissertation (1956) of Trenchard More, a pupil of C. E. Shannon. On the basis of the work of Kanger and myself, thereupon D. Prawitz, H. Prawitz and

N. Voghera (1958)[16] worked out a 'program' for an electronic computer (the Facit EDB of the AB Åtvidabergs Industrier of Stockholm) by which it is possible to instruct this machine to carry out deductions in the predicate calculus. A number of simple deductions have been carried out by the machine. The speed attained is as yet much too low to consider practical applications by means of the machines available at present. This however will be different as soon as one (a) has simplified the deduction methods enough, and (b) has at his disposal automata of a still greater speed and capacity which are, moreover, better adapted to the particular demands to be asked of a 'logical machine'.

(ij) A. Newell and H. A. Simon (1956)[17] and starting from their work H. Gelernter (1957)[18] have likewise drawn up programs for logical deductions. They, however, work with the relatively cumbersome deduction methods current before 1955. They aim at heightening the efficiency of the 'logical machine' by incorporating in the program, besides the deduction methods chosen, also a certain 'heuristics'. To that purpose one could on the one hand go out from the results from an investigation into the heuristic expedients man uses in looking for a proof; I mention in this connection the work of G. Polya.[19] On the other hand one could, by looking *directly* for a 'heuristics' suitable for the machine, perhaps obtain a deeper insight in the course of logical thinking in man. So here is the possibility of a connection with thought psychology. The investigations of Newell and Simon are more particularly directed to laying this connection.

Personally I am not inclined to except many results of this search for an heuristic suitable for the machine. Namely, I have observed in my own investigations that with application of the semantic tableau method (for the related deduction methods of Hintikka, Kanger and Schütte the same, of course, holds) deductions came about comparable to those which are brought forth spontaneously by logical thinking. The heuristic of human thought, therefore, seems to have been incorporated already fairly completely in the new deduction methods.

However this may be, we seriously have to take the possibility into account that in the near future we can entrust the search for logical deductions to electronic machines. The question arises of course what the further consequences of such a development will be.

In answering this question one must presuppose that the work, notably of a mathematical investigator, indeed consists for a very important part in looking for logical deductions. The automatization of this work, by the way, is completely in the line of a development which first, by the introduction of suitable notations, has led to a great simplification of numerical calculation and subsequently by the construction of suitable machines to its automatization.

The cancellation of an important part of the normal daily work of the mathematical investigator can be expected to necessitate a shift in his attention. In the first place he will have to develop a certain "heuristic", to provide the machine with the necessary problems regularly. Moreover he will have to learn to bring the problems into the form most suitable for the machine (the actual 'programming', in which the instructions are translated into a code 'understandable' for the machine, is now already completely in the hands of specialists). He is no longer preoccupied with the separate theorems, but he will have to incorporate the structure of a mathematical entity as an entirety. In brief, his work will more and more start to resemble the work conducted now already on the margin of actual mathematics, in the area of mathematical foundational studies.

One should now already consider the possibility of an adaptation of the practice of and notably the instruction in mathematics to needs which will perhaps be already felt at rather short notice.

(4) The development of mathematical logic has stimulated work in the field of *history of logic*; it has, as I have already observed, thrown a completely new light on all kinds of subtleties in older logic for which, under the influence of later trivializing and psychologizing tendencies, proper understanding had been lost. The extremely destructive critique on the logic of antiquity and the Middle Ages, by writers like Barthélemy Saint-Hilaire, A. Franck and C. Prantl (in A. A. Virieux-Reymond, *La logique et l'épistémologie des stoïciens* [20], one finds some characteristics references) in fact is replaced by deep admiration in A. Reymond, H. Scholz and J. Łukasiewicz.

I think this admiration is in all respects deserved, also with regard to the pioneer work conducted by these scholars but that does not detract from the fact that I feel that notably the interpretations defended by Łukasiewicz and Scholz are on numerous points open to refinement and correction. I mention the characterization (also contested by G. H. von

Wright in his *Logical Studies*[21]) of the Aristotelian and stoic logic, respectively as a system of laws and a system of rules, the conception of Aristotle's exposition method (about which more in an *Appendix*), the explanation of Kant's distinction between analytic and synthetic judgements, the attribution to Bolzano of the semantic method. So very much remains yet to be done.

In the area of medieval logic many important texts have been published not at all or insufficiently. L. M. de Rijk has, during the last years, made highly important contributions with his edition of Petrus Abaelardus and Garlandus Compotista[22].

The meaning of the history of logic in the wider context of a philosophical study of contemporary logic lies, among other things, in the fact that it arms us against an overestimation of the importance of the artificial and conventional elements in mathematical logic. This point is perhaps sufficiently illustrated by reference to the discussion about Eubulides *cornutus*. I should nevertheless be glad if this Academy decided in due time to publish my work on the history of logic.

(5) For a philosophical study of logic, on the basis of similar considerations, further knowledge of the *logic of non-Western cultures* could also be important. At this point I of course depend on secondary sources and I have to admit that I have been able to find only very little which was useful for my standpoint. An exception is the investigation on Indian logic by St. Schayer, A. Kunst and D. Ingalls (about which more information is given by Bocheński in his *Formale Logik*) which, I hope, will be continued by J. F. Staal.

This less satisfactory state of affairs can of course be explained. The historians and orientalists who would have to inform us have, understandably, only rarely the logical schooling necessary for an adequate treatment of the extremely tricky problems which arise in this connection.

Therefore I am happy to take this opportunity to make some methodological remarks. In my opinion in the investigation of a logic of a non-Western culture one would have to ask in the first place the following questions: (i) Has the culture in question produced a theory of formal logic? (ij) In the culture in question does formal logical reasoning occur? (iij) Does the language of the culture in question give suitable means of expression for formal logical reasoning?

I would like to illustrate these questions in depth and subsequently make some supplementary remarks.

(i) Naturally one can *a priori* expect no similarity of such a theory with the formal logical theories known to us in the Western tradition; moreover one should be prepared for the possibility that the treatment of formal logical problems is combined or mingled with considerations of another, for example, epistemological, psychological or grammatical nature.

(ij) One also should be prepared for the possibility that the formal logical reasoning is governed by other rules than the ones current for us in this connection, and that it is combined or mingled with other forms of argumentation.

(iij) In the first place one will have to pay attention to the availability of equivalents for the means of communication common to us for *negation*, *implication*, (if..., then), *generalization*, the *modalities* and for semantical concepts such as *true* and *false*. Besides that one has to take into account the possibility that in formal logical reasoning, or possibly in the description and analysis thereof, an appeal is made to other logical and semantic concepts than are current with us.

Although I have, as I said, only very few useful data over the (formal) logic of the non-Western cultures at my disposal, it would still surprise me very much if, after closer investigation, it would turn out that one of these cultures had produced a formal logic which on the one hand in range and rigor of construction would be comparable to the logic of antiquity and the Middle Ages, and which, on the other hand, would be characterized by strongly divergent logical concepts and logical rules. Such a state of affairs would be difficult to rhyme with the circumstance that in the elementary arithmetical concepts and insights such a striking divergence is not demonstrable.

To be sure one has often tried to make the existence of such a divergence plausible on the basis of linguistic or race-psychological considerations. Such arguments, which are usually strongly influenced by insights originating from the psychologizing phase of logic, are not very convincing, however. The race-psychological considerations are refuted by the observation that already in the development of the logic of antiquity and the Middle Ages thinkers of many nationalities and races have combined, while contemporary logic finds practitioners over the whole world.

In fact the linguistic arguments look somewhat stronger to me. It is very plausible that some languages are more suitable than others as a medium of logical thought. But we have seen that even Greek was not a perfect medium, so that already Aristotle had to infringe on the rules of normal usage. With such tricks undoubtedly the languages of other cultures could also be made a suitable medium for logical thinking.

The large-scale development of logic since its entry into the mathematizing phase has made it suitable for many kinds of applications, both on the theoretical and the practical level; but this development at the same time threatens to alienate philosophy. For philosophy, as a result, the danger arises that irrational tendencies – already an influence to be reckoned with in contemporary thinking – become predominant; it would thereby in the long run start to lose its intended character of rational reflection.

Therefore I argue that logic, even in its mathematizing phase, should remain both instrument and object of philosophical reflection.

APPENDIX

A modern analysis of a syllogism in the modus CELARENT:

> No human being rides on horseback over the rooftops
> All saints are human beings
> _____
> ∴ No saint rides on horseback over the rooftops

(further on it will become sufficiently clear that I did not choose this example just for fun) can perhaps clarify somewhat the general tenor of Aristotle's answer to Eubulides (the method applied I have elucidated more amply in my communication on *Semantic Entailment and Formal Derivability*). If we represent the premises and conclusion respectively by the formulas:

$$(1) \quad \overline{(Ex) \, [M \, (x) \, \& \, P \, (x)]}$$
$$(2) \quad (y) \, [H \, (y) \rightarrow M \, (y)]$$

and:

$$(3) \quad \overline{(Ez) \, [H \, (z) \, \& \, P \, (z)]}$$

then the above reasoning corresponds to the following semantic tableau:

True	False	
(1) $\overline{(Ex)\,[M\,(x)\,\&\,P\,(x)]}$	(3) $\overline{(Ez)\,[H\,(z)\,\&\,P\,(z)]}$	
(2) $(y)\,[H\,(y)\rightarrow M\,(y)]$	(4) $\overline{(Ex)\,[M\,(x)\,\&\,P\,(x)]}$	
(5) $(Ez)\,[H\,(z)\,\&\,P\,(z)]$	(10) $M\,(a)\,\&\,P\,(a)$	
(6) $H\,(a)\,\&\,P\,(a)$		
(7) $H\,(a)$	(11) $H\,(a)$	
(8) $P\,(a)$		
(9) $H\,(a)\rightarrow M\,(a)$	(13) $M\,(a)$	(14) $P\,(a)$
	(12) $M\,(a)$	

We can now convert this tableau into the following formal deduction in a System of Natural Deduction.

(1)	$\overline{(Ex)\,[M\,(x)\,\&\,P\,(x)]}$	[prem 1]
(2)	$(y)\,[H\,(y)\rightarrow M\,(y)]$	[prem 2]
	-----------------	
(5)	$(Ez)\,[H\,(z)\,\&\,P\,(z)]$	[+ hyp 1]
	= = = = = = = = =	
(6)	$H\,(a)\,\&\,P\,(a)$	[+ hyp 2]
(7)	$H\,(a)$	(6)
(8)	$P\,(a)$	(6)
(9)	$H\,(a)\rightarrow M\,(a)$	(2)
(12)	$M\,(a)$	(7), (9)
(10)	$M\,(a)\,\&\,P\,(a)$	(8), (12)
	= = = = = = = =	
(4)	$\overline{(Ex)\,[M\,(x)\,\&\,P\,(x)]}$	[– hyp 2]
	-----------------	
(3)	$\overline{(Ez)\,[H\,(z)\,\&\,P\,(z)]}$	[– hyp 1]

We can also formulate this reasoning adequately and without much trouble by means of ordinary language.

Given: (1) No human being rides on horseback over the roof tops. (2) All saints are human beings.

To prove: (3) No saint rides on horseback over the roof tops.

Proof: We make use of the method of proof by contradiction. We assume for that purpose: (5) There are saints who ride horseback over the rooftops; take, for the sake of convenience, more in particular: (6) Sinterklaas is a saint who rides on horseback over the rooftops. It then holds that: (7) Sinterklaas is a saint, and: (8) Sinterklaas rides on horseback over the rooftops. On the basis of (2) it further holds that: (9) If Sinterklaas is a saint, then he is a human being. From (7) and (9) we deduce by means of *modus ponens*: (12) Sinterklaas is a human being. Because of (8) and (12) we get next: (10) Sinterklaas is a human being who rides on horseback over the rooftops. That we have considered Sinterklaas in particular apparently is of no importance, so that independently of assumption (6): (4) There are human beings who ride on horseback over the rooftops. But that is contrary to (1), so that assumption (5) is absurd. Therefore: (3) No saint rides on horseback over the rooftops, as was to be proved.

I now consider the conclusion of Aristotle's argument (*De sophisticis elenchis*, cap. xxii, $178^b36–179^a10$).

Also ⟨the previous conclusions hold for the argument⟩ that there is a third man, besides man as such and the separate human beings. Because man, like each *universale*, means not a *particulare*, but a *quale*, or a *relativum*, or something of that nature. So it is likewise with the question: are Koriskos and Koriskos, the musician, one and the same or different? Because the first means a *particulare*, and the second a *quale*, so that it is not possible that it is exposed; for, not the fact that it is exposed makes the third man appear, but its recognition as a *particulare*. Because there cannot be a *particulare* which is both Kallias and the human being. But if somebody says that the exposed is not a *particulare* but a *quale*, than there is no problem; because then there will be a certain unity besides the many particular things, for example man. Therefore it can evidently not be admitted that that which is pertained in a universal way to all things would be a *particulare*, but one has to maintain that it has to mean a *quantum* or a *quale* or a *relativum* or something of that nature.

This exposition becomes understandable if we bring it into connection with the analysis of a syllogism such as I have just given. The term 'Koriskos, the musician' in Aristotle corresponds to the parameter 'a' in the above semantic tableau and to the term 'Sinterklaas' in its informal reproduction. The question as to the *ontological status* of the *denotatum* of such terms has been asked repeatedly in the course of history. It arises here in connection with the transition from (5) to (6), which is characteristic for Aristotle's *method of exposition*, and gives to this method a problematic character; on analogous discussions by Frege, von Meinong and Russell one finds some information in Bocheński's *Formale Logik*.

As to the question whether this *denotatum* has to be designated as a *particulare* or as a *universale* Aristotle faces, as is clear from the quoted text, an extremely difficult dilemna.

1. If we assume, as everyone in the first instance will be inclined to, that 'Sinterklaas' denoted a *particulare* and therefore functions as a *proper name*, then we immediately encounter the difficulty, as was evident from the analyzed reasoning, that an actual bearer of this proper name cannot exist as a concrete person. Bishop Nicholas of Myra was, in fact, a saint, but he did not ride on horseback over the roof tops. Now one can take recourse in the supposition that Sinterklaas is to be considered as an ideal person. i.e. *the saint that rides over the roof tops on horseback par excellence*. But, Aristotle very rightly remarks, that leads to the acceptance of Plato's Theory of Ideas. Doubtlessly Eubulides had reproached him because his exposition method implied an appeal to the Theory of Ideas, and therefore would have to lead to the antinomy of the Third Man. This explains the emphasis with which Aristotle points to the fact that in applying the exposition method, the exposed term should *not* be conceived as a denotation of a *particulare*.

2. We can also consider the term 'Sinterklaas' as a *generic name*; it then obviously serves as a denotation of the general concept: *saint who rides horseback over the roof tops*. If he accepts this interpretation, Aristotle gets entangled in other difficulties, however. For from the analyzed reasoning it is clear that the term thus conceived is 'empty', so that its introduction is inconsistent with the principles of Aristotle's syllogistics.

From the contemporary standpoint there is no objection against introducing 'empty' terms, so that the term 'Sinterklaas' can, if so desired, be taken as a generic name. In that case, however, we would have to review the analyzed reasoning rather severely; it loses thereby its 'natural' character.

Happily the objections against the conception of 'Sinterklaas' as a proper name are not insurmountable, either, from the contemporary standpoint. Should we assume that this proper name serves as a denotation of *the saint who rides over the roof tops on horseback par excellence*, then the analyzed reasoning only makes an appeal to the supposition:

If there is one saint who rides over the roof tops on horseback, then it is Sinterklaas.

This supposition can be held as true, even if we identify Sinterklaas with Bishop Nicholas of Myra. Indeed, an implication with a false antecedent, according to contemporary logic, has to be designated as true.

This discussion yields a partial justification of a conception of Łukasiewicz, formerly contested by me, according to which Aristotle explained the exposed term as a denotation of a *universale*. In my opinion we should, however, distinguish at this point in Aristotle's doctrine three phases of development.

1. Initially the exposed term was, as is in any case the most obvious course, and as in mathematical proofs is always done, interpreted as a proper name. The existence of this phase, in itself already plausible, has to be assumed to explain the discussions about the interpretation; this phase must have fallen in a period in which Aristotle was still strongly under the influence of Plato's Theory of Ideas.

2. Subsequently the exposed term was conceived of as a generic name. This phase is represented by the text quoted. We can assume that Eubulides' polemic against Aristotle's syllogistics fell in this phase and had more or less the following tenor:

(I) The conception of the exposed term as a proper name means an appeal to Plato's Theory of Ideas, and therefore leads to the antinomy of the Third Man;

(II) The exposed term therefore must be considered as a generic name; this conception, however, forces admittance of 'empty' terms;

(III) Admission of 'empty' terms makes, in the context of Aristotle's syllogistics, reasonings possible like the *cornutus*, which, starting from true premises, yield false conclusions;

(IV) Therefore Aristotle's syllogistics, because of its appeal to the exposition method, is untenable.

3. Finally Aristotle, perhaps under the influence of Eubulides' critique, abandoned the exposition method altogether. This is apparent from the fact that Aristotle, as Łukasiewicz remarks[23], in the final chapter of

Book I of the *Analytica priora*, where he gives a survey of syllogistics, no longer appeals to the exposition method. Also in accordance with this interpretation is the fact that Alexander of Aphrodisias rejects the exposition method as 'not syllogistic'. Galenus, on the other hand, as K. Berka has observed[24], does use this method; he apparently takes the exposed term as a generic name.

Perhaps Aristotle's difficulties are partly connected with the circumstance that he, as Łukasiewicz observes, does not completely understand the nature of *hypothetical reasoning*. Such an hypothetical reasoning arises, for example, when we consider from the analyzed reasoning the part consisting of the propositions (2), (5), (6), (7), (8), (9), (12), (10), and (4) independently. Now in this hypothetical reasoning only the term 'Sinterklaas' plays a role, and in the restricted context of this reasoning, there is no reason whatsoever to consider this term as 'empty'; to the contrary, by virtue of supposition (5) this term is *not* empty. The fact that *after* the final conclusion (4) of the hypothetical reasoning is obtained, the supposition (5) is rejected as absurd, cannot detract from the conclusive character of the hypothetical reasoning as such.

This short discussion may also illustrate the importance of the need mentioned before to disengage in the application of Aristotle's *analytical method* certain parts of an argument from the wider context. That the consistent application of this principle invalidated Eubulides' objections, Aristotle apparently did not observe.

That Aristotle's immediate successors Eudemus and Theophrastus, as well as somewhat later the stoic logicians paid particular attention to the hypothetical reasonings, was, indeed, completely justified. Apparently only the Stoics have completely understood the consequences of entirely upholding '*two-valuedness*'.[25]

NOTES

[1] E. W. Beth [U].
[2] L. Wittgenstein [1].
[3] K. R. Popper [1].
[4] W. V. Quine [4].
[5] E. W. Beth [79].
[6] I. M. Bocheński [1].
[7] [Port-Royal] *La logique ou l'art de penser* (nouvelle éd., Paris 1816).

[8] K. Marbe [1].
[9] E. W. Beth [U].
[10] P. F. Strawson [1].
[11] S. Feferman and R. L. Vaught [1].
[12] R. C. Lyndon [1].
[13] J. M. Le Blond [1].
[14] H. G. Apostle [1].
[15] K. J. J. Hintikka [1]–[3], S. Kanger [1], K. Schütte [1], [2].
[16] D. Prawitz, H. Prawitz en N. Voghera [1].
[17] A. Newell and H. A. Simon [1].
[18] H. Gelernter [1], H. Gelernter and N. Rochester [1].
[19] G. Polya [1], [2].
[20] A. Virieux-Reymond [1].
[21] G. H. von Wright [1].
[22] L. M. de Rijk [1], [2].
[23] J. Łukasiewicz [1].
[24] K. Berka [1].
[25] See in connection with this chapter also: Beth [108], [126], [V], [W], [S], [94], Bocheński [2], Dijksterhuis [1], McCulloch and Pitts [1], Quine [1], Robinson [1], Sassen [1], Wedberg [1], Wittgenstein [2].

Annotation. Presumably E. W. Beth [V] and [W].

CHAPTER X

CONSTANTS OF MATHEMATICAL THOUGHT

1. CAPTATIO BENEVOLENTIAE

To begin with I would like to state in a few words on what grounds I have decided to bring up the announced subject matter in this meeting. I deem this topic not only important for mathematics and to the exact sciences associated with it by long tradition, but also for general philosophy and for the humanities. Thus the following considerations open up to the possibility of constructing a *philosophical logic* as E. Husserl[1] hoped, although this construction will in many respects have to take a different course than the one conceived by this philosopher.

Moreover these considerations will, I hope, be able to give us a certain insight into the philosophical background of what I will designate as *mathematical linguistics*: I think thereby, other than of the somewhat older work of R. Carnap[2], mainly of the investigations of N. Chomsky.[3] I fully realize, of course, that what mathematical linguistics has thus far achieved in no way satisfies the legitimate demands of the professional linguists.[4] For a fair judgement of the results already achieved, and especially for a correct estimate of the possibilities for development which still exist, it is, however, absolutely necessary that one also is fully aware of the philosophical background.

When, in the following, I attempt as much as possible to leave out of consideration all the details of the specific logical-mathematical 'technique', then one is pleased not to see in that a misdirected attempt at vulgarization; as a philosopher I consider the restrictions which I impose on myself here and elsewhere as fundamentally desirable. In a scientific technique there is almost always an arbitrary element, and a philosophical discussion which puts too much stress on the 'technical' aspects of the problem in question, exposes itself all to easily to the suspicion of resting for a part on purely arbitrary stipulations.

In my desire for an exposition which is as elementary as possible, I feel strengthened by the fact that various trends of thought which, usually in very 'technical' dressing, play an important role in modern mathematical foundational studies, can be found already in a more primitive form in the Greek philosophers. I allude here to the so-called 'sophisms' which often strongly offended earlier generations; their deeper sense has only been rediscovered in the last decades.[5]

On the other hand an analysis of these reasonings, in the light of the interpretation now become possible, can form a very valuable substitute for a direct exposition of the corresponding contemporary ideas.

That in the following there can hardly be any expectation of completeness goes without saying.

2. PHASES OF THE DEVELOPMENT OF MATHEMATICAL THOUGHT

In the following I will classify the developments of mathematical thought in four phases, which I denote as empirical mathematics, naive mathematics, critical mathematics, and abstract mathematics.

By *empirical mathematics* I mean various mathematical insights concerning actions like counting, measuring, weighing, and calculating, which, for the time being, remain bound to the concrete context in which they are initially given and which therefore remain scattered over various areas of application: architecture, geodesy, finance, navigation, astronomy and so on. Already in the pre-Greek civilizations an impressive total of mathematical insights finds expression in many ways.

Naive mathematics represented by Euclid's *Elements* has an intuitive and elementary character; the concept formation is not yet very exact, and already because of that the proofs cannot be very rigorous, either. The links with the world of experience have been broken, however; in antiquity, especially Plato pointed out the importance of this step. Aristotle holds more affection for applied mathematics, but he, too, appears completely familiar with the conception of a pure mathematics as it came to flourish in old Hellas.

This distinction between pure and applied mathematics was not maintained when, in more recent times, mathematics was put in the service of the budding natural sciences. If we pay attention to the increase in the extent of mathematical knowledge, then we can undoubtedly speak of a new period of bloom; if at the same time we take into account the degree of methodic rigor, then we observe a striking decline in comparison with what had been attained already by the Greeks.[6]

Critical mathematics originated because, in the long run, pure mathematics asserted itself again after all, and mathematical research looked for new ways without continually paying heed to the concrete needs of the areas of application. In the course of the 18th century a striking interest arose for more speculative problems, like those concerning the theory of parallels and the infinitesimal calculus.

Abstract mathematics originated around 1850 as a result of the introduction of problems which I will describe later in more detail.

3. PHILOSOPHICAL BACKGROUND

The problems characteristic for a philosophy of mathematics throughout the ages, are for an important part, based on the peculiar discrepancy which exists between mathematical truths on the one hand and mathematical objects on the other. The mathematical truths belong to those ingredients of human knowledge to which we are used to ascribing the highest degree of clarity, certainty and evidence; but in the world of our experience we look in vain for the mathematical objects to which these truths apply. We are, for example, certain of the fact that two arbitrarily chosen points determine a straight line which contains them both; but in the world of our experience we never encounter points or straight lines in the sense of the geometric terminology.

A first solution to the problem posed here we can derive from *platonism*. It is important in this connection that this doctrine postulates the existence of points and straight lines in the transcendental world, to which even the human soul has belonged before it was banished to the material world. Our geometric knowledge rests on our memories of this pre-existence.

In this primitive form the solution presented by platonism is unsatisfactory. It is true that it explains the absence of mathematical objects in our present world of experience, but at the same time it makes our certainty with regard to our mathematical knowledge completely incomprehensible. Indeed, how can this knowledge, which rests on memories from an earlier existence, have a higher degree of certainty than the knowledge which relies on observations in the present?

The viewpoint of *aristotelianism* is more plausible in this regard. Here it is postulated that the mathematical objects exist *in* the objects of the world of our experience, from which they, so to say, are distilled by an act of '*abstraction*'.[7] From this standpoint the certainty of mathematics is, to a certain extent, comprehensible; moreover, and that is where the particular value of aristotelianism lies, it accounts for the possibility of applying mathematics in the empirical sciences. However, it does not explain the results mathematicians obtain in the investigation of various highly complicated objects for which, in the world of our experience, no material correlate can be found.

In explanatory power neither platonism nor aristotelianism is a match for *constructivism*, a viewpoint which has the idealistic tendency in common with platonism. According to this conception mathematical objects are constructs of the human mind itself. Constructivism, which we already encounter with Plotinus and Nicholas of Cusa, makes mathematical knowledge into a form of self-knowledge.

It is remarkable, and at the same time characteristic for the after effect of scholastic thought, that Descartes, who with so much emphasis had pointed out the significance of self-knowledge, nevertheless held to an aristotelian conception of mathematical thought. Only in Hobbes, whose way of thinking in many respects is close to cartesianism, do we rediscover mathematical constructivism.

It is surprising that Hobbes' conception of mathematics has become the originating point for Vico's ideas about the science of history, and at the same time has gone on to form one of the most important and characteristic ingredients of Kant's philosophy of the mathematical sciences. Thus the dualism in the methodology of the neokantians from Baden originates with the mathematical constructivism of Plotinus, Cusanus and Hobbes, which has developed on the one hand with Kant to a theory of the *nomothetic*, and on the other hand with Vico to a theory of the *ideographic sciences*; without a doubt an instructive example of the unexpected results to which an historical development can lead.

Although mathematical constructivism has, mainly because of Kantianism, obtained a strong influence on the philosophical conceptions concerning mathematical thought, it has only in the most recent times, with Brouwer and his school, directly affected mathematical research itself. The case of Kepler, who refused to recognize the existence of a regular heptagon as long as for such a figure no construction had been given, remained for centuries completely unique.[8]

4. MATHEMATICAL MONISM, ABSTRACT MATHEMATICS AND THE PROBLEM OF FOUNDATIONS

The objects studied by the Greek mathematicians had still kept so much similarity with material objects that Aristotle could defend the doctrine already discussed according to which mathematical objects are obtained by '*abstraction*' from material objects. I now want to sketch the developments by which this doctrine has become untenable.[9]

These developments are initiated by the introduction of *analytic geometry* by P. Fermat and R. Descartes, by which a fusion of mathematics and analysis was effected; following this course one has in our time come to a complete unification of pure mathematics. The traditional ties of certain parts of pure mathematics to their specific areas of application have thereby been cut off definitively. The consequence of this is a radical reduction of the mathematical objects, which are not only placed outside of the world of experience, but are at the same time stripped from their intuitive intent; that is what one aims at if one designates contemporary pure mathematics as *abstract mathematics*.

Already early one came to the insight that the tenability of the procedure characteristic for abstract mathematics was bound to certain conditions; in particular one had to

(i) in the formulation of axiomata, the introduction of definitions and the derivation of theorems take heed of the most rigorous demands of methodical exactness, and

(ij) answer the question to which objects mathematical truth really pertained. The full weight of these demands has probably been appreciated for the first time by G. Frege; it is subsequently impressed on the mathematicians thoroughly again by the occurrence of the paradoxes. The totality of the problems which are raised by the endeavor to satisfy these demands, is denoted as the *problem of foundations*.

In the treatment of this problem, the opinions have, as is well-known, strongly diverged. For our purpose it is sufficient to distinguish four directions: *logicism* and *cantorism* which together continue the tradition of *platonism*, and *intuitionism* and *formalism* which should be considered as variants of *constructivism*.

5. CONSTANTS OF MATHEMATICAL THOUGHT

It will benefit the clarity of my argument if I now, already, without any more motivation, clarify, by means of a simple listing, what I consider to be the constants of mathematical thought. I mention then as such:
  1. the *algorithm*,
  2. the *deductive method*,
  3. the *infinite*.
Algorithms we encounter already in empirical mathematics; it is just the presence of algorithms which gives us the right to designate it as mathematics. In Greek mathematics, to the contrary, little attention was paid to algorithms because one thought them worthy only of a place in applied mathematics. The development of algebra also brought rehabilitation for the algorithms.

It was the introduction of the deductive method which enabled Greek mathematics to rise above the level of empirical mathematics. This is even more remarkable because, according to contemporary insight, Greek mathematicians mastered the deductive method only partially.

The infinite also plays an important role in Greek mathematics, although it is known that the Greek mathematicians handled the infinite somewhat diffidently, and that they had the tendency to camouflage the occurrence of the infinite in mathematics as much as possible. The basis for that has to be sought in the fact that the incomplete mastery of the deductive apparatus by the Greek mathematicians made them practically powerless against the paradoxes to which reasoning about the infinite turns out only too easily to lead.

It is indeed understandable that the mathematicians encountered great difficulties when the development of the infinitesimal calculus made it impossible to camouflage the significance of the infinite for mathematics any longer. Critical mathematics in fact distinguishes itself from naive mathematics by a more complete mastery of the deductive apparatus which makes possible reasoning about the infinite without constantly reverting into paradoxes.

Critical mathematics therefore distinguishes itself from naive mathematics *not* by the occurrence of new constants, and for abstract mathematics the same holds with respect to critical mathematics. Abstract mathematics differs from critical mathematics mainly because it is serious about the question as to the nature and the existence of mathematical objects; at this point critical mathematics liked to orient itself to tradition, but that is not satisfactory now the unification of pure mathematics has been achieved.

The deductive structure apparently has to be considered as a very essential characteristic, and not merely a 'technical' incident. A philosophical discussion about mathematics will therefore also have to extend to its deductive apparatus, to *logic*.

6. THE SORITES

To obtain a concrete base for the exposition of some views concerning the foundation and construction of abstract mathematics, I give here a modernized version of a sophism ascribed to Eubulides of Milete, which is closely related to an argument originating with A. Tarski.[10]

Let K be the (infinite) class, formed by the following premisses U_1, $U_2, ..., U_m, ...$:

(U_1) the set A contains at least one element,

(U_2) the set A contains at least 2 elements,

....

(U_m) the set A contains at least m elements,

.... *etc. ad inf.*

We now ask the question of the conclusion:

(V) the set A contains infinitely many elements,

follows logically from this class of premisses.

This question can, through the establishment of criteria for *following logically*, be specified in different ways, and admits according to the chosen specification different answers. In fact, we consider here only two criteria:

CRITERION I. The conclusion V follows logically from the premiss class K, if *each* set A which satisfies all premisses, $U_1, U_2, ..., U_m, ...$ in K at the same time satisfies the conclusion V.

CRITERION II. The conclusion V follows logically from the premiss class

K, if there is a (sound[11]) argument which starting from the premises in K yields the conclusion V.

By argument we have to understand in this connection a *finite* sequence of propositions which starts with the premises, and which for the rest consists of a number of consecutive conclusions $V_1, V_2, ..., V_{k-1}, V_k, ..., V_n$ such that V_k is each time an immediate consequence of the premises combined with the previous conclusions $V_1, V_2, ..., V_{k-1}$, while V_n coincides with the desired end-conclusion V.

We now observe in the first place that criterion II makes *at least as heavy* requirements as criterion I in the sense that if criterion II is satisfied, then criterion I will also always be satisfied. Indeed, imagine that criterion II *is* satisfied but criterion I is *not*.

Because criterion I is not satisfied, there has to be a set A which does fulfill all premises $U_1, U_2, ..., U_m, ...$, but *not* the conclusion V; with regard to this set A all these premises are therefore *true*, but the conclusion *false*.

Because on the other hand, according to supposition, criterion II is satisfied, there has to be a finite sequence of propositions as just described. This supposed reasoning, however, proceeds from *true premises* U_1, $U_2, ..., U_k$ but yields a *false* conclusion V, so that it cannot be designated as sound; therefore criterion II cannot have been satisfied. Our supposition, therefore, turns out to be absurd and therefore criterion II makes at least as heavy requirements as criterion I.

It is now a curious fact, however, that secondly, criterion II makes really *heavier* requirements than criterion I. In the case we consider, namely criterion I *is* satisfied, but criterion II is *not*.

We first apply criterion I. So let A be a set which fulfills *all* premises $U_1, U_2, ..., U_m, ...$. Then A has to contain at least one element, at least 2 elements, ..., at least m elements, ... etc. ad inf. But then A apparently has to contain infinitely mainly elements, and thus has to fulfill conclusion V. This holds for *each* set A as considered and therefore criterion I is satisfied.

We now consider criterion II. Assume that a reasoning as required by this criterion exists. Such a reasoning is a *finite* sequence of propositions and therefore would look like this:

$$U_1, U_2, ..., U_{67}, V_1, V_2, ..., V_{83}, V.$$

But we will never be able to recognize such a reasoning as sound. The premisses U_1, U_2, ..., U_{67} do not even guarantee that the set A contains at least 68 elements; let alone that the set A contains infinitely many elements. There can therefore exist no reasoning as required by criterion II, and therefore this criterion is not satisfied.

We can formulate the conclusion of our argument as follows: although in the sense of criterion I the conclusion V follows logically from the premiss class K, it is not possible to derive the conclusion V in the sense of criterion II from the premiss class K by means of a sound reasoning.

7. CONSEQUENCES

This conclusion affirms in the first place the necessity to specify for the deductive method involved the fundamental concept *follows logically*, in particular with respect to the occurrence of the *infinite*. The two criteria we have considered correspond to two conceptions of the infinite which are long known as the *actual* and the *virtual infinite*.

In criterion I the premiss class K, and with that also the set A, is presented as a completely given entity, as actual infinite. In criterion II on the other hand the premiss class K is presented as being created by the continuous adjoining of new premisses U_m; at the same time the set A is created in a similar way; here we meet the virtual infinite.

The process by which the premiss class K is each time enriched by a premiss U_m has the character of an *algorithm*. This character applies equally to the process (the reasoning or logical deduction) by which from the premiss class K each time new conclusions are obtained in the sense of criterion II.

This brief consideration gives us a certain insight into the aims and right to existence of three sectors of contemporary foundational studies.

The want of a specification of the concept *follow logically* and, more in general, the transition to modern abstract mathematics, in which mathematical reasoning loses its hold on all kinds of empirical and intuitive data, necessitates an extremely careful investigation of the deductive apparatus. One must say that this has first been recognized by G. Frege who has indeed made very important contributions to the modern so-called *mathematical logic*. Thanks to the investigations in this area we have at present at our disposal a very accurate description of the current deductive apparatus.

We can, completely in the spirit of Cantor, characterize the general abstract set theory developed by him as a *mathematical theory of the actual infinite*. One has, as is well-known, since Aristotle raised various objections against the possibility of such a theory, and it is remarkable that even Georg Cantor himself initially had an unquiet conscience and felt the need to seek the advice of theologians. His diffidence is even in our time still comprehensible for who sees the grand perspectives opened by set theory and who envisualizes the grandiose constructions which are enabled by it.

One commonly attributes to Cantor's set theory a strongly *platonistic* character. One has thereby more in mind, however, than merely the already-discussed reduction of the mathematical objects by which they are not only placed outside our concrete world of experience, but also stripped of all intuitive content.

If in the connection of abstract set theory one speaks of *platonism*, then one means with that in particular the aim to '*compress*' a set which in the first instance is commonly given as a multiplicity of objects which all fulfill a certain condition (or which all have a certain characteristic property in common) to one single object that, in its turn, can also serve as an element of a set.

If one, however, as Cantor and his first supporters did, applies this '*compression*' of multiplicities completely without restriction, then it turns out that one reverts into paradoxes.[12] To avoid these paradoxes one has to restrict the possibility of '*compression*' in an appropriate way; this has led to the construction of axiom systems for set theory.

Just as mathematical logic, set theory also initially encountered much resistance, but in the course of the years it has become current almost everywhere. Nevertheless it leaves room for what one can designate as a *mathematical theory of the virtual infinite*. This studies more in particular those sets of which the elements can be produced by means of a suitable algorithm. An example of such an algorithm is presented by the premiss class K, considered before, but also the class C of all conclusions V which can be derived from the premiss class K by logical reasoning can be mentioned as an example.

8. THEORY OF ALGORITHMS

This theory has been developed in the years around 1930 by a number of logicians and mathematicians independently of each other in rather divergent versions which, however, afterwards turned out to be equivalent.[13] I give here a very brief summary of the theory of algorithms proposed by E. L. Post.[14]

This theory deals, roughly said (I will give presently a somewhat more accurate description), with the formation of certain sets of (finite) *sequences of signs* consisting of *signs a, b, c, ...* which belong to a certain (finite) *alphabet* $\{a, b, c, ...\}$. Certain sequences of signs are beforehand given by way of *axioms*, the others are obtained as *theorems* from the axioms by (finitely many times) repeated application of certain *productions*. Thus each algorithm determines a certain subset of the set of *all* sequences of signs which could be obtained from the signs of its alphabet.

A certain algorithm is apparently unambiguously characterized by the following data:

1. a finite alphabet $\{a, b, c, ...\}$,
2. one or more axioms,
3. one or more productions.

I will now first give some concrete examples. Arbitrary sequences of signs will thereby be denoted as $u, v, w, x, y, z, ...$.

EXAMPLE 1. Let the algorithm A be characterized by:

1. the alphabet $\{a, b\}$;
2. the axioms a and b;
3. the production $u \Rightarrow ua$ and $u \Rightarrow ub$.

Let N_1 be the set of all sequences of signs which can be obtained by the application of this algorithm. Then according to 1. the set N_1 can contain exclusively sequences of signs consisting only of signs a and b. According to 2. N_1 contains to start with the signs of sequences a and b, each consisting of one sign only.

Under 3. we now find the rule according to which the further elements of N_1 can be produced. If a sequence of signs u has been obtained as an element of N_1, then we can also always add to N_1 the sequences of signs ua and ub as elements.

We can, in other words, extend an already obtained sequence of signs always arbitrarily by tacking on a sign a or b. It is easy to see that the algorithm A_1 determines the set N_1 of *all* finite sequences of signs consisting only of signs a and b.

The application of a production consists, stated more accurately, of the fact that we replace the variable u everywhere where it occurs by one and the same, otherwise chosen arbitrarily, sequence of signs. If in that way on the left side of the $\Rightarrow$-symbol an axiom or an already obtained theorem occurs, then also the sequence of signs on the right side of the $\Rightarrow$-symbol is recognized as a theorem. We will execute this for

EXAMPLE 2. Let the algorithm A_2 be characterized by:
1. the alphabet $\{a, b\}$;
2. the axioms ab and ba;
3. the productions $ub \rightarrow uba$ and $ua \rightarrow uab$.

Consecutively then the elements of the set N_2 determined by A_2 appear in the right column of the table below.

production $ub \Rightarrow uba$	production $ua \Rightarrow uab$	N_2
u: a $ab \Rightarrow aba$	*u: b* $ba \Rightarrow bab$	(1) *ab* [ax]
(1) *ab* ∴ *aba* (3)	(2) *ba* ∴ *bab* (4)	(2) *ba* [ax]
u: ba $bab \Rightarrow baba$	*u: ab* $aba \Rightarrow abab$	(3) *aba*
(4) *bab* ∴ *baba* (5)	(3) *aba* ∴ *abab* (6)	(4) *bab*
u: aba $abab \Rightarrow ababa$	*u: bab* $baba \Rightarrow babab$	(5) *baba*
(6) *abab* ∴ *ababa* (7)	(5) *baba* ∴ *babab* (8)	(6) *abab*
u: baba $babab \Rightarrow bababa$	*u: abab* $ababa \Rightarrow ababab$	(7) *ababa*
(8) *babab* ∴ *bababa* (9)	(7) *ababa* ∴ *ababab* (10)	(8) *babab*
u: ababa $ababab \Rightarrow abababa$	*u: babab* $bababa \Rightarrow bababab$	(9) *bababa*
(10) *ababab* ∴ *abababa* (11)	(9) *bababa* ∴ *bababab* (12)	(10) *ababab*
u: bababa $bababab \Rightarrow babababa$	*u: ababab* $abababa \Rightarrow abababab$	(11) *abababa*
(12) *bababab* ∴ *babababa* (13)	(11) *abababa* ∴ *abababab* (14)	(12) *bababab*
		(13) *babababa*
		(14) *abababab*

The algorithm A_2 determines a set N_2 which contains again exclusively sequences of signs consisting of the signs a and b; to begin with N_2 contains the sequences of signs ab and ba.

According to 3. we can extend a sequence of signs already obtained only in such a way that we have a b follow an a and an a follow a b. The set N_2 therefore contains just those sequences of signs which consist of two or more signs and in which two equal signs never occur next to each other.

EXAMPLE 3. Let the algorithm A_3 be characterized by:
1. the alphabet $\{a, b\}$;
2. the axioms a, b, aa, and bb;
3. the productions $uv \Rightarrow auv$, $uv \Rightarrow buv$, $uv \Rightarrow uva$, $uv \Rightarrow uvb$.

According to 3. we can only extend sequences of signs consisting of two or more signs. Our algorithm A_3 evidently determines the set N_3 or $N_1 - N_2$ of all the sequences of signs which belong to N_1 but not to N_2.

EXAMPLE 4. Let the algorithm A_4 be characterized by:
1. the alphabet $\{a, b\}$;
2. the axiom ab;
3. the production $u \Rightarrow aub$.

This algorithm determines the set N_4 of those sequences of signs which consist of a certain number of a's followed by an equal number of b's.

EXAMPLE 5. Let the algorithm A_5 be characterized by:
1. the alphabet $\{a, b\}$;
2. the axioms aa and bb;
3. the productions $u \Rightarrow aua$ and $u \Rightarrow bub$.

To this algorithm the set N_5 corresponds of all sequences of signs which are constructed from a sequence of signs u followed by the mirror-image of u.

EXAMPLE 6. Let the algorithm A_6 be characterized by:
1. the alphabet $\{a, b\}$;
2. the axioms aa and bb;
3. the productions $uu \Rightarrow uaua$ and $uu \Rightarrow ubub$.

The corresponding set N_6 contains all the sequences of signs which consist of a sequence of signs u followed by the same sequence of signs u.

EXAMPLE 7. Let the algorithm A_7 be characterized by:
1. the alphabet $\{a, b, \rightarrow\}$;
2. the axiom $a \rightarrow a \rightarrow a$;
3. the productions $u \Rightarrow b \rightarrow u$ and $a \rightarrow a \rightarrow u \Rightarrow u$.

The corresponding set N_7 consists of formulas of the types:

$$b \rightarrow b \rightarrow \ldots \rightarrow b \rightarrow a, \quad \text{and};$$
$$b \rightarrow b \rightarrow \ldots \rightarrow b \rightarrow a \rightarrow a \rightarrow a.$$

It would lead me too far astray if I would attempt to outline sharply what is admissible as a production.[15] A reference to the characteristic examples 1–7 should suffice, whereby I want to draw attention to the fact that, of course, much more complicated algorithms are possible. The alphabet can contain more than three signs and the axioms can be more numerous and complicated. In the productions two or more variables $u, v, \ldots$ can occur and moreover on the left side of the $\Rightarrow$-symbol two or more premisses can occur.

Example 7 differs from the previous ones because here a production

$$a \to a \to u \Rightarrow u$$

occurs which leads to shortening. We cannot exclude such productions, because we also want to conceive of formalized deductive theories as algorithms. In such a theory commonly *modus ponens*:

If U, then V,

U

$\therefore V$

occurs, which in the corresponding algorithm would lead to a production:

$$u, u \to v \Rightarrow v$$

In connection with the examples 1–7 the terms '*axiom*' and '*theorem*' were used in an improper sense. They reobtain their actual sense when they are used in relation to those algorithms which correspond to deductive theories; this application at the same time explains the terminology used.

9. DECIDABLE AND CANONICAL

In this section we restrict ourselves to the consideration of algorithms with the alphabet $\{0, 1\}$; this does not mean an essential restriction.[16]

Let N be the set of all finite sequences of signs consisting of the digits 0 and 1. Such a sequence of signs can, as is well known, be taken as a notation in the *binary system*, of one of the natural numbers $0, 1, 2, 3, \ldots$[17]. For the sake of convenience we will identify in this section each sequence of signs with the natural number for which it yields the notation so that we can designate these as sequences of signs as natural numbers.[18] We are now going to occupy ourselves with the question in which way we can characterize a set of natural numbers, i.e. a subset of N.

(1) An obvious method, very much in use, consists of characterizing a subset N_1 of N by means of a criterion which allows a decision for any

natural number n whether it belongs to N_1 or not. Let, for example, N_1 be the set of all even numbers; then the sequence of signs n belongs to N_1, if and only if the last digit in the sequence is a 0.

This example is, of course, extremely simple. But it is clear that there has to exist a great variety of criteria (or *decision procedures*), so that also a great variety of subsets N_1 of N can be characterized in the manner here described; these subsets N_1 of N are known as *decidable* (or *recursive*).

From the famous incompleteness theorems of Gödel and others, it now follows, however, that not all subsets N_1 are decidable; that is to say: there are subsets N_1 which in no way can be characterized by means of a decision procedure. This brings us to the question if there is also a method which enables us to characterize a non-decidable set N_1.

(2) We now observe that certain subsets N_1 of N can be characterized by means of a suitably chosen algorithm with alphabet $\{0, 1\}$. The sets which can be obtained in this manner are designated by Post as *canonical sets*. These canonical sets, each characterized by a well-described step-wise generation of its elements show, in my opinion, a certain intuitive relationship with the virtual infinity of Aristotle.

One could presume that *each* subset N_1 of N is canonical, but we shall soon see that this is not the case; the following is true however:

I. Each decidable set N_1 is *a fortiori* canonical; I won't go into the proof of this theorem.

Now one could think that, the other way around, each canonical set N_1 would be decidable, too; to support this opinion one could then perhaps reason as follows. Let n be a natural number (given as a sequence of signs); we look for an answer to the question whether n belongs to the set N_1 or not. To that purpose we employ the algorithm belonging to N_1 so that consecutively all natural numbers belonging to N_1 are produced. If n occurs in this manner, then we have thereby an affirmative answer to the question; if n on the other hand does not occur, then the answer has to be negative.

This argument however holds no water. An affirmative answer to the question will indeed come to light in the manner described. Should the answer, on the other hand, be negative, then we can only each time again observe that n has still not occurred; but with that, in general, no guarantee is obtained that n won't occur at some future time. In other words: an algorithm is in general no decision procedure.

That the presumption described here is, in fact, incorrect is clear from:

II. There is a set N_1 which is canonical, but not decidable; the proof of this theorem is given by Post directly, by the construction of an algorithm B_1 which determines a suitable set N_1.

Now suppose, however, that both the set N_1 and its complement $N - N_1$ are canonical; let n be a natural number about which is asked whether it belongs to N_1 or not. We can now at the same time start the algorithm B_1 belonging to N_1 and the algorithm B'_1 belonging to $N - N_1$. As n belongs to either N_1 or to $N - N_1$, n must be produced either by B_1 or by B'_1. In any case n must therefore occur, and thereby a guarantee is given that the question about n will be answered. We therefore have:

III. If a canonical set N_1 has a canonical complement $N - N_1$, then the set N_1 is decidable.

Now one could presume that each non-decidable set is at least canonical; that this presumption is incorrect is expressed by:

IV. There is a canonical set N_1 with a non-canonical complement $N - N_1$.

The proof of this theorem can be given as follows. Let N_1 be a canonical non-decidable set; according to II there is such a set. Assume that the complement $N - N_1$ is also canonical; then according to III the set N_1 would be decidable, contrary to supposition. Thus $N - N_1$ is not canonical, as was to be proved.

In summary we can observe that sets of natural numbers are afflicted with different degrees of complexity. The most simple ones are the *decidable* (or *recursive*); these can be characterized by means of a decision procedure.

More complicated are the *canonical* (or *recursively enumerable*) sets; these cannot (in general) be characterized by means of a decision procedure, but they can be characterized by means of an algorithm. A third class is formed by the *complements* of canonical sets; in general these can be characterized neither by means of a decision procedure nor by means of an algorithm. Sets of this last class are therefore in general very difficult to handle.

S. C. Kleene (1943) and A. Mostowski (1946) have shown that these three mentioned classes are by no means the end of the matter. It turns out that there exists an infinitely proceeding 'hierarchy' of classes formed by sets of a higher and higher degree of complexity.

Although the theory of algorithms derives its origin from questions of a predominantly speculative character, connected with problems in the foundations of mathematics, it has besides its significance for mathematics and philosophy, quickly obtained a certain practical importance in connection with the spectacular development in the area of the electronic calculating machines.

It is true that its significance in this respect lies not so much in the fact that it gives direct instructions for the construction of calculating automata. It rather presents general points of view and directions and in particular gives an insight into the fundamental limits which by nature are put to a meaningful usage of calculating automata.

But there is still a particularly close connection between algorithms and calculating automata: *an algorithm is* like *a calculating automaton on paper.*

In other words: for a given algorithm one can always devise a calculating automaton that automatically effectuates the desired productions; and with a given calculating automaton one can always devise an algorithm, the productions of which are just given by that calculating automaton.

So the theory of algorithms is at the same time a *theory of calculating automata* in so far as it is abstracted from all specifically technical problems.

10. MATHEMATICAL LINGUISTICS

As I have already remarked in par. 1 it is in no way my intention to make a plea here for mathematical linguistics, as it has been developed notably by N. Chomsky. The task I put myself to here is more restricted; I hope to show that the work of Chomsky and his supporters can be more adequately understood and judged more justly if one takes into account its background, as this is more in particular formed by the ideas which are discussed in summary in par. 8 and 9.

Let E be the set of all finite sequences of words occurring in the English language, and let E_1 be the subset of E consisting of all grammatical English sentences. We now put ourselves to the problem of *characterizing the set* E_1.

The most obvious approach now is to attempt to characterize the set E_1 by means of a suitably chosen decision procedure. There is nothing new in such an attempt; each English grammar of the old-fashioned normative type will give us criteria which allow us to decide for each arbitrary sequence of words w whether it belongs to E_1 or not.[19] It is however, if I am not mistaken, a generally recognized fact that even the very best grammar remains very far-removed from this ideal.

Naturally explanations of this fact are in no way lacking. One adduces, for example, that it would not be practical to aspire for absolute completeness. Furthermore one points out that the English language is continuously subject to various partly very elusive changes. Also one draws the attention to the desirability of a certain tolerance with regard to individual variations in the matter of usage of and feeling for language.

I want to underline here again that I do not put myself to the task of making a judgement of explanations as meant here. I do want to draw attention to the fact that the considerations in par. 9 put at our disposal a completely new principle of explanation. A characterization of the set E_1 of all grammatical English sentences by means of a grammar of the current type is only possible if this set E_1 is decidable.

The difficulties which the construction of an ideal English grammar of the current type appear to present could be an indication that the set E_1 is not decidable.

In this negative form the new explanation does not, of course, make us much wiser. On the basis of the previous section we can accord to this explanation a more positive tenor by supplementing it with the assumption that *the set* E_1 *of all grammatical English sentences is canonical*. Such a canonical set is in general too complicated to be decidable; we can nevertheless deal with it constructively and master it rationally because we can think of the sequences of words w belonging to it as being produced by a suitably chosen algorithm.

Therefore we consider the hypothesis according to which the set E_1 of all grammatical English sentences is *canonical* (and *not decidable*) in somewhat more detail. If this hypothesis is right, then the current ideal of an

English grammar is not capable of realization. Such a grammar cannot be cast in the stereo-typed forms, but will, for example, have to consist of a description of an appropriate algorithm. On the other hand once one has constructed an appropriate algorithm, then one has thereby demonstrated the correctness of the hypothesis.

Now, as it occurs to me, Chomsky's work can freely be characterized as an investigation into the possibility of such an algorithm. What is denoted by Chomsky as a '*model*' or as a '*grammar*' comes very close to an algorithm in the sense of Post; I presume that systems like Chomsky's can in general be transferred into the forms prescribed by Post. In this connection I will just mention that I have adopted the examples 4–6 in par. 8 directly from Chomsky.[20]

The idea that an approach like Chomsky's would entail a trivialization of the investigation of language is completely unfounded. To the contrary: Chomsky's methods open up a possibility of giving an adequate description of grammatical structures which are too complicated to be dealt with by means of a grammar of the current type.

11. REICHLING'S CRITIQUE ON CHOMSKY

As supplementation and illustration I would like to make a few remarks about the critique levelled against Chomsky's ideas by A. Reichling.[21] I have thereby in no way the intention of defending Chomsky, but I would like to contribute something to a better understanding.

In the first place a general remark. It appears to me that Reichling ascribes to Chomsky a dogmatism that is not present in his work, and that he has too little eye for the experimental way in which Chomsky works with his algorithms. If we start from the idea that there are good grounds for the search for an algorithm as described in par. 10, then we have to agree that such an algorithm will have to be enormously complicated. So there is everything to be said for restricting oneself for the time being to the construction and investigation of more simple algorithms corresponding to formalized languages or to efficiently chosen 'sub-languages' of English.

In various forms Reichling[22] reproaches Chomsky "that he presupposes the complete English grammar in his manipulations". This reproach is difficult to rhyme with Chomsky's express appeal to "a partial knowledge".[23] Presumably there is a misunderstanding in play here which could be based on an incorrect interpretation of phrases like: "a grammar generates all grammatically 'possible' utterances".[24]

What is meant here can be illustrated on the basis of Chomsky's words: "Assuming the set of grammatical sentences of English to be given."[25] With regard to this set, namely, a similar problem arises as stated by Reichling with relation to his own system and to von Humboldt's *'innere Sprachform'*.[26]

In par. 10 I have suggested an analogy between the sets E and E_1 on the one hand and the sets N and N_1 introduced in par. 9 on the other; this analogy is however by no means complete. N and N_1 are purely mathematical entities, and as such given *a priori* (the problems inherent to this being given *a priori* are of no concern in this connection). The sets E and E_1 on the other hand have not been given *a priori*; they are, however, not given in the world of our experience either. So if we want to say something about these sets anyway, then we will just have to *assume* them as being given.

On the basis of this supposition we can now speak about the sets E and E_1 as about well-determined entities, even if for the time being we know them only as vaguely outlined by our 'partial knowledge'. Only the construction of a suitable algorithm accords the necessary definiteness to the sets E and E_1.[27]

According to Reichling[28], Chomsky has made "a methodical blunder ...: he lets ... the rules of language be potentially derived with the aid of and with an eye on a method adopted from other sciences, among which is electronic engineering". I can only understand his reproach as an expression of a methodical purism that I have always found particularly unfruitful and that is now really out of date. With approval I now quote here Chomsky[29]: "... we shall never consider the question of how one might have arrived at the grammar. ... Questions of this sort are not relevant to the program of research that we have outlined above. One may arrive at a grammar by intuition, guesswork, all sorts of partial methodological hints, reliance on past experience, etc.".

Chomsky[30] writes: Similarly, consider such pairs as

(113)   (i) the picture was painted by a new technique
         (ii) the picture was painted by a real artist.

These sentences are understood quite differently, though identically represented as NP − was + Verb + en − by + NP on the level of phrase structure. But their transformational history is quite different.

In connection with this Reichling[31] writes:

"And so, Chomsky says, their transformational *history* is quite different, and therefore we understand them completely differently. ...

"Is this right, or rather: has this been proven?"
and he answers[32]:

"Chomsky's first basic linguistic mistake is that he supposes without a semblance of a proof that the transformational *history* of an expression could lead the understanding of a language user. Indeed, this presupposes that the language user knows this history in some way or another. For that, however, there has never been any evidence."

The '*therefore*' that Reichling means to read and for which he finds no proof is however nowhere written in Chomsky. A passage like the following,[33] however, points in the direction of Reichling's interpretation:

"To understand a sentence, then, it is first necessary to reconstruct its analysis on each linguistic level; ..."

From the context, and anyhow from the whole tendency of Chomsky's work,[34] it is clear, however, that 'understanding' cannot refer to the intuitive 'understanding of a language user'. In the earlier quoted passage Chomsky[30] merely observes that the difference which according to the reactions of the language users exists between the sentences (i) and (ii), but which has to stay unnoticed on the level of the 'phrase structure' can be made 'visible' by means of a closer look at the transformational history of both.

According to Reichling's opinion[35] Chomsky's method can "in the end not yield a grammar for linguists, but perhaps the basis for a program for electronical technicians which would turn out to work more accurately than the existing programs. Only, these two aims are not exactly the same."

I believe we have to present the matter somewhat differently. Grammars of the current type have originally been constructed for the practical language user; subsequently more scientific (more complete and accurate) versions have become current to serve linguists.

So one can also imagine that grammars in the spirit of Chomsky in the first place have to help realize a practical purpose like automatic translation; it is then reasonable to expect that here, too, in the long run more scientific versions will arise to serve the linguists. However: a practically useful grammar, in the spirit of Chomsky, has to fulfill the highest requirements in the matter of completeness and accuracy; for they will have to be used by an automaton and will therefore have to be '*foolproof*'. One will therefore have to use all available scientific data in its construction and it is for that reason not very meaningful to develop afterwards again a more scientific version for the linguists.

I have already said before that it is not my intention to plead here for the ideas and the work of Chomsky. That the now available grammars in the sense of Chomsky cannot measure up to the best grammars of the traditional type can hardly be doubted. In particular it can be said that the transformational method has not been developed in a satisfactory way. On the other hand one has to observe that if the hypothesis stated in par. 10 is correct, then the possibilities for development of traditional grammar in contrast to those of the grammar in the spirit of Chomsky will be very restricted in the future.

I would like to give a somewhat less colored judgement than Reichling does.[36] Doubtlessly Chomsky has undergone the influence of N. Goodman and W. V. Quine. There is also every indication to classify these thinkers as logical positivists; for that purpose one will have to take logical positivism in a wider sense than as just a continuation of the doctrine of the Vienna Circle. Chomsky, however, will have drawn at least as much inspiration from mathematical logic, mathematical foundational studies, and information theory.

12. CONCLUSION

Reichling's fierce critique on the work and method of Chomsky is, in my opinion, essentially a protest against the expansion of mathematical thought as it has manifested itself on a large scale in the last decades. It would not be correct, however, to charge such a protest to the very wide spread fear of mathematics. I believe that the motive must looked for, rather, in the apprehension of a certain denaturation of the sciences in question as a consequence of undesirable influences emanating from other areas of science. That this motive plays an important role in Reichling is evident from his appeal already cited to a methodological purism and from the remarks he sometimes makes about physicalism and logical positivism.[37]

Even rather recently such an apprehension was by no means unfounded. As long as mathematics was closely allied to one of its areas of application, i.e. the inorganic sciences, its application in other areas indeed led only too easily to an unwarranted influencing by physics and subsequently by materialistic metaphysics.

At the moment, however, there is no ground at all for an apprehension for such an indirect influence of physics or a materialistic metaphysics on the humanities. In fact, as I argued in par. 4 pure mathematics has, after 1850, emancipated itself progressively from its areas application. Since then its development has been more and more determined by internal problems, and in particular by the problem of foundations. Thus the theory of algorithms, which I have discussed briefly, is the result of such an autonomous development inside of pure mathematics, independent of applications in the area of science.

Because of this development a sharp light came to rest on the importance of certain basic concepts which I have designated in par. 5 as *constants of mathematical thought*:

1. the *algorithm*,
2. the *deductive method*,
3. the *infinite*.

To these basic concepts three mathematical disciplines correspond which, in the totality of unified mathematics, take a central place:

1. the *arithmetic of natural numbers*,
2. *mathematical logic*,
3. *abstract set theory*.

In my opinion these three disciplines will, provided they are given sufficient thought, be able to take the place E. Husserl[38] had intended for a *philosophical logic*, but which he himself was never able to fill satisfactorily.

Valuable contributions to the philosophical reflection desired here have been made by such thinkers as R. Carnap[39] and W. V. Quine[40]; I am also active in this field myself. To the problems which usually come up for discussion in this connection belongs the question about the relations between the formalized languages used in mathematical logic and common usage. Of great importance, for example, is the question to what extent the results of mathematical logic, which, in the first instance relate to the deduction inside certain formalized languages, can also be binding for reasoning in terms of ordinary language; a negative answer to this last question seems obvious, but it is nevertheless remarkable that the so-called problem of *Locke-Berkeley*, which came up within traditional logic and epistemology, has only been completely cleared up on the basis of mathematical logic.[41] A philosophical reflection to lead to a philosophical logic will, of course, also have to consider the intuitionistic critique on classical logic and mathematics.

Naturally in no way do I cherish the illusion that a philosophical reflection as I have pleaded above will in the long run lead to a more or less unanimously accepted solution to the problems which come up here. One does not reach such a unanimity in other areas of philosophical reflection.

The prospect that many fundamental differences of opinion will continue to exist should, however, never induce one to undervalue the great clarification which could be reached on a great number of points, and which in some cases has already been attained.

NOTES

[1] E. Husserl [1], 1. Bd., p. 252.

[2] R. Carnap [1], [2].

[3] N. Chomsky [1].

[4] A. Reichling [1].

[5] E. W. Beth [U], pp. 20–25.

[6] F. G. Backbier [1].

[7] E. W. Beth [U], pp. 18–20.

[8] J. Kepler, *Harmonices mundi* L. I.; comp. E. Cassirer [1], 1. Bd., p. 379; E. W. Beth [H], p. 267.

[9] For more data see E. W. Beth [89].

[10] E. W. Beth [U], pp. 21–22.

[11] The concept *sound* will not be described in more detail here, but is characterized in the sequel of the argument indirectly; comp. further Chapter I.

[12] See p. 95. Comp. E. W. Beth [U], pp. 147–148.

[13] E. W. Beth [W], pp. 89–90.

[14] This theory is most easily accessible in the exposition given by P. C. Rosenbloom [1], Chapter IV; comp. A. A. Markov [1].

[15] A sharp description is given by P. C. Rosenbloom [1], p. 162.

[16] Roughly, one sees this easiest if one just thinks of the fact that each text can be written by means of the Morse alphabet.

[17] That each natural number possesses more than one notation (0 digits completely on the left, if any, don't contribute to the numerical value) doesn't matter here.

[18] It is common to neglect in this connection the distinction between 'use' and 'mention' of a symbol.

[19] This point has first been broached by Y. Bar-Hillel in 1953; comp. Y. Bar-Hillel [1].

[20] N. Chomsky [1], p. 21.

[21] A. Reichling [1].

[22] A. Reichling [1], pp. 69, 70, 89.

[23] N. Chomsky [1], p. 14.

[24] N. Chomsky [1], p. 48.

[25] N. Chomsky [1], p. 18.

[26] A. Reichling [1], p. 77.

[27] N. Chomsky [1], pp. 13–14.

[28] A. Reichling [1], p. 79.

[29] N. Chomsky [1], p. 56.

[30] N. Chomsky [1], p. 89.

[31] A. Reichling [1], p. 85.

[32] A. Reichling [1], p. 87.

[33] N. Chomsky [1], p. 87.

[34] N. Chomsky [1], p. 48.

[35] A. Reichling [1], p. 91.

[36] A. Reichling [1], p. 90.

[37] A. Reichling [1], pp. 11, 55–56, 90. – In this connection the discussion of the influence of logical positivism on the *glossematics* of L. Hjelmslev in G. Ungeheuer [1] also deserves to be mentioned. Although this exposition is not completely unassailable – for example, it doesn't keep *logical positivism, logicism* and *logistics* (*mathematical logic*) sufficiently apart – it is considerably more adequate than the considerations in B. Siertsema [1]; comp. about this last work F. J. Whitfield [1].

[38] E. Husserl [1].

[39] R. Carnap [1], [2].

[40] W. V. Quine [2], [3].

[41] E. W. Beth [94]; also comp. Chapters IV, VIII and IX.

SOURCES

I. *Fundamental Criterion for the Soundness of Arguments.* – Par. 2–6 have been taken with some changes from the article 'Moderne logica', *Euclides* **34** (1958/59), published by P. Noordhoff N.V., Groningen.

II. *Inferential and Classical Logic.* – The par. 8–12 have, with some changes, been taken from 'Operatieve en semantische fundering van de logica', presented among other times at the Genootschap voor wetenschappelijke philosophie, October 21, 1961, and taken up in *Annalen* **33** (1961/62), see *ANTW* **54** (1961/62).

III. *Proof by Contradiction.* – For the main part written especially for this book.

IV. *The Problem of Locke-Berkeley.* – Presented under the title 'Het expositorisch syllogisme', on University Day, October 20, 1956, in Amsterdam.

V. *About the So-Called Thought Machine.* – With some changes taken from a lecture given in Amersfoort and published in the anthology *Mens en computer; automatie, industriële en culturele revolutie*, Uitgeverij Het Spectrum, Aulareeks 136, Utrecht and Antwerp, 1965.

VI. *The Paradoxes.* – Drastically revised version of 'L'état actuel du problème logique des antinomies', communicated at the Congrès international de philosophie des sciences (Paris, October, 1949) and printed in Fasc. II: *Logique*, Paris, 1951.

VII. *Reason and Intuition.* – Presented at the Genootschap voor wetenschappelijke philosophie, October 24, 1953, and taken up in *Annalen* **23** (1953/54), see *ANTW* **46** (1953/54). Also appeared separately with Van Gorcum & Comp. N.V., Assen, 1954.

VIII. *Formalized Languages and Normal Usage.* – Presented at the Genootschap voor wetenschappelijke philosophie, November 16, 1957 and taken up in *Annalen* **29** (1957/58), see *ANTW* **50** (1957/58).

IX. *Considerations about Logical Thinking.* – *Mededelingen Kon. Ned. Akad. van Wet., Afd. Lett.* **N.R. 23**, Nr. 1 (1960).

X. *Constants of Mathematical Thought.* – *Mededelingen Kon. Ned. Akad. van Wet., Afd. Lett., N.R.* **26**, Nr. 7 (1963).

BIBLIOGRAPHY

A. WORKS FROM OTHER AUTHORS

Apostle, H. G.: [1] *Aristotle's Philosophy of Mathematics*, Chicago 1952.

Backbier, F. G.: [1] *Wiskunde in dienst van de Natuurwetenschap*, Thesis, University of Utrecht, Utrecht 1960.

Bar-Hillel, Y.: [1] 'Decision Procedures for Structure in Natural Languages', *Logique et Analyse* N.S. 2 (1959).

Berka, K.: [1] 'Der "Beweis durch Heraushebung" bei Galenos', *Phronesis* 3 (1958).

Bernays, P.: [1] 'Die Erneuerung der rationalen Aufgabe', in *Proceedings of the Tenth International Congress of Philosophy*, Amsterdam 1949.

Bocheński, I. M.: [1] *Formale Logik*, Freiburg/München 1956; [2] 'Spitsfindigkeit', in *Festgabe an die Schweizerkatholiken*, Freiburg, Schweiz 1954.

Bolland, G. J. P. J.: [1] *De ruimtevoorstellingen*, Batavia 1889.

Bouligand, G. and Desgranges, J.: [1] *Le déclin des absolus mathématico-logiques*, Paris 1949.

Carnap, R.: [1] *Logische Syntax der Sprache*, Wien 1934; [2] *Studies in Semantics* I–II, Cambridge, Mass. 1942–1943.

Cassirer, E.: [1] *Das Erkenntnisproblem*, Vol. 1, 2nd. Ed., Berlin 1911.

Chomsky, N.: [1] *Syntactic Structures*, 's-Gravenhage 1957.

Church, A.: [1] 'Schröder's Anticipation of the Simple Theory of Types', *J. of Unified Science* 9 (1940) [to my knowledge appeared as a preprint only].

Curry, H. B.: [1] 'The Interpretation of Formalized Implication', *Theoria* 25 (1959).

Desgranges, J.: see: Bouligand, G. and Desgranges, J.

Dijksterhuis, E. J.: [1] *De Elementen van Euclides*, 2 Vols., Groningen 1929–1930.

Dürr, K.: [1] 'Aussagenlogik im Mittelalter', *Erkenntnis* 7 (1938/39); [2] *The Propositional Logic of Boethius*, Amsterdam 1951.

Feferman, S. and Vaught, R. L.: [1] 'The First Order Properties of Products of Algebraic Systems', *Fundamenta Mathematicae* 47 (1959).

Frege, G.: [1] *Die Grundlagen der Arithmetik*, Breslau 1884.

Gelernter, H.: [1] 'Theorem Proving by Machine', in *Summaries of Talks Presented at the Summer Institute of Symbolic Logic in 1957 at Cornell University* (mimeographed).

Gelernter, H. and Rochester, N.: [1] 'Intelligent Behavior in Problem-Solving Machines', *IBM Journal of Research and Development* 2 (1958).

Gentzen, G.: [1] *Recherches sur la déduction logique*, translated and commented by R. Feys and J. Ladrière, Paris 1955.

Goblot, E.: [1] *Traité de logique*, Paris 1918.

Gödel, K.: [1] *The Consistency of the Axiom of Choice and of the Generalized Continuum Hypothesis with the Axioms of Set Theory*, Princeton 1940; [2] 'Russell's Mathematical Logic', in P. A. Schilpp (ed.), *The Philosophy of Bertrand Russell*, Evanston, Ill. 1946: [3] 'What is Cantor's Continuum Problem?', *Amer. Math. Monthly* 54 (1947).

Goodman, N. and Quine, W. V.: [1] 'Steps Toward a Constructive Nominalism', *JSL* **12** (1947).

Hasenjaeger, G.: see: Scholz, H. and Hasenjaeger, G.

Hermes, H. and Scholz, H.: [1] 'Mathematische Logik', *Enzykl. der math. Wiss.*, Vol. I 1, Nr. 1, Part 1, Leipzig 1952.

Heyting, A.: [1] *Intuitionism, an Introduction,* Amsterdam 1956.

Hintikka, K. J. J.: [1] 'A New Approach to Sentential Logic', *Societas Scientiarum Fennica, Commentationes physico-mathematicae,* Vol. 17, Nr. 12 (1953); [2] 'Notes on Quantification Theory', *ibid.,* Vol. 17 Nr. 2 (1955); [3] 'Two Papers on Symbolic Logic', *Acta Philos. Fennica,* Vol. 8, Helsinki 1955.

Hölder, O.: [1] *Die mathematische Methode,* Berlin 1924.

Husserl, E.: [1] *Logische Untersuchungen,* 2. Ed., Halle 1913.

Jevons, W. Stanley: [1] *Pure Logic and Other Minor Works,* London 1890.

Kanger, S.: [1] *Provability in Logic,* Stockholm 1957.

Kazemier, B. H.: [1] 'De geformaliseerde leugenaar', *ANTW* **45** (1952/53).

Laer, P. H. van: [1] 'De definitie van het begrip "meetkundige plaats"', *Euclides* **28** (1952/53).

Le Blond, J. M.: [1] *Logique et méthode chez Aristote,* Paris 1939.

Linsky, L.: [1] 'Meaning and Use', *ANTW* **53** (1960–61).

Lorenzen, P.: [1] 'Ein dialogisches Konstruktivitätskriterium', in *Infinitistic Methods,* Proceedings of the Symposium on Foundations of Mathematics, Warsaw, 2–9 September 1959, Warszawa 1961.

Löwenheim, L.: [1] 'On Making Indirect Proofs Direct', translated by W. V. Quine, *Scripta Math.* **12** (1946).

Łukasiewicz, J.: [1] *Aristotle's Syllogistic from the Standpoint of Modern Formal Logic,* Oxford 1951.

Lyndon, R. C.: [1] 'An Interpolation Theorem in the Predicate Calculus', *Pacific Journal of Mathematics* **9** (1959).

Marbe, K.: [1] *Experimentell-Psychologische Untersuchungen über das Urteil. Eine Einleitung in die Logik,* Leipzig 1901.

Maritain, J.: [1] *Petite logique,* 11th Ed., Paris 1933.

Markov, A. A.: [1] *Theory of Algorithms,* Jerusalem etc. 1961.

Martin, R. M.: [1] *Toward a Systematic Pragmatics,* Amsterdam 1959.

Masterman, M.: [1] 'Metaphysical and Ideological Language', in C. A. Mace (ed.), *British Philosophy in the Mid-Century,* London 1957.

McCulloch, W. C. and Pitts, W.: [1] 'A Logical Calculus of the Ideas Immanent in Nervous Activity', *Bull. of Math. Biophysics* **5** (1943).

McNaughton, R.: see: Wang, Hao and McNaughton, R.

Moody, E. A.: [1] *Truth and Consequence in Mediaeval Logic,* Amsterdam 1953.

Newell, A. and Simon, H. A.: [1] 'The Logic Theory Machine', *IRE Transactions on Information Theory,* Vol. IT–2, Nr. 3 (1956).

Nuchelmans, G.: [1] 'Betekenissystemen', *ANTW* **50** (1957/58); [2] 'De waarheidsparadox en de gewone taal', *ANTW* **50** (1957/58).

Olbrechts-Tyteca, L.: see: Perelman, Ch. and Olbrechts-Tyteca, L.

Perelman, Ch. and Olbrechts-Tyteca, L.: [1] *Traité de l'argumentation,* Paris 1958.

Pitts, W.: see: McCulloch, W. C. and Pitts, W.

Polya, G.: [1] *How to Solve It,* 2nd Ed., New York 1957; [2] *Mathematics and Plausible Reasoning,* 2 Vols., Princeton, N.J., 1954.

Popper, K. R.: [1] 'The Trivialization of Mathematical Logic', in *Proceedings of the*

Xth Int. Congress of Philosophy, Amsterdam 1949.

Prawitz, D., Prawitz, H. and Voghera, N.: [1] *A Mechanical Proof Procedure and Its Realization in an Electronic Computer* (mimeographed), Stockholm 1959.

Quine, W. V.: [1] 'Mr. Strawson on Logical Theory', *Mind* N.S. **62** (1953); [2] *From a Logical Point of View*, Cambridge, Mass., 1953; [3] *Word and Object*, Cambridge, Mass. 1960; [4] *Methods of Logic*, revised Ed., New York 1959; see: Goodman, N. and Quine, W. V.

Reichling, A.: [1] *Verzamelde studies*, Zwolle 1961.

[Rijk, L. M. de, ed.]: [1] 'Petrus Abaelardus', *Dialectica*, Assen 1956; [2] 'Garlandus Compotista', *Dialectica*, Assen 1959.

Robinson, A.: [1] 'Proving a Theorem (as Done By Man, Logician, or Machine)', in *Summaries of Talks Presented at the Summer Institute of Symbolic Logic in 1557 at Cornell University* (mimeographed).

Rochester, N.: see: Gelernter, H. and Rochester, N.

Rosenbloom, P. C.: [1] *The Elements of Mathematical Logic*. New York 1950.

Russell, B.: [1] *The Principles of Mathematics*, Vol. I, London 1903; [2] *Introduction to Mathematical Philosophy*, London 1919; [3] 'The Cult of "Common Usage"', *British J. Philos. of Science* **3** (1952/53); see Whitehead, A. N. and Russell, B.

Sassen, F.: [1] *Geschiedenis van de wijsbegeerte in Nederland tot het einde der negentiende eeuw*, Amsterdam-Brussels 1959.

Scholz, H.: [1] *Metaphysik als strenge Wissenschaft*, Cologne 1941; see: Hermes, H. and Scholz, H.

Scholz, H. and Hasenjaeger, G.: [1] *Grundzüge der mathematischen Logik*, Berlin-Göttingen-Heidelberg 1961.

Schopenhauer, A.: [1] *Die Welt als Wille und Vorstellung*, Leipzig 1819.

Schütte, K.: [1] 'Ein System des verknüpfenden Schliessens', *Archiv für Mathematische Logik und Grundlagenforschung* **2** (1956); [2] *Beweistheorie*, Berlin 1960.

Siertsema, B.: [1] *A Study of Glossematics*, Thesis, University of Amsterdam, The Hague 1955.

Sigwart, Chr.: [1] *Logik*, Vol. 2, 5th Ed., Tübingen 1924.

Simon, H. A.: see: Newell, A. and Simon, H. A.

Strawson, P. F.: [1] *Introduction to Logical Theory*, London-New York 1952.

Tarski, A.: [1] 'The Semantic Conception of Truth and the Foundation of Semantics', *PPR* **4** (1944); [2] *Introduction to Logic and to the Methodology of Deductive Sciences*, 2nd Ed., New York 1946; [3] 'A Problem Concerning the Notion of Definability', *JSL* **13** (1948); [4] *Logic, Semantics, Metamathematics*, Papers from 1923 to 1938, Oxford 1956.

Ubbink, J. B.: [1] 'Waarneming, bewering en logische redenering', *ANTW* **47** (1954/55).

Ungeheuer, G.: [1] 'Logischer Positivismus und moderne Linguistik (Glossematik)', *Uppsala Universitets Årsskrift* 1960 **11** (1960).

Vaught, R. L.: see: Feferman, S. and Vaught, R. L.

Virieux-Reymond, A.: [1] *La logique et l'épistémologie des stoïciens*, Chambéry 1949.

Voghera, N.: see: Prawitz, D., Prawitz, H. and Voghera, N.

Vredenduin, P. G. J.: [1] 'Grenzen van de formaliseerbaarheid', *ANTW* **45** (1952/53).

[Wallies, M., ed.]: [1] *Alexandri in Aristotelis Analyticorum priorum librum I commentarium*, Berolini 1883.

Wang, Hao and McNaughton, R.: [1] *Les systèmes axiomatiques de la théorie des ensembles*, Paris-Louvain 1953.

Wedberg, A.: [1] *Plato's Philosophy of Mathematics*, Stockholm 1955.

Weersma, H. A.: [1] 'Bezwaren tegen H. Scholz' Metaphysik als strenge Wissenschaft', *ANTW* 39 (1946/47).
Whitehead, A. N. and Russell, B.: [1] *Principia Mathematica*, 3 Vols., 2nd Ed., Cambridge 1925–1927.
Whitfield, F. J.: [1] review of Siertsema, B. [1]) *Language* 31 (1955).
Wittgenstein, L.: [1] *Tractatus Logico-Philosophicus*, with a translation by C. K. Ogden, 2nd. Ed., New York-London 1933; [2] *Remarks on the Foundations of Mathematics*, Oxford 1956.
Wright, G. H. von: [1] *Logical Studies*, London 1957.

B. WORKS OF E. W. BETH

[E²]   *Geschiedenis der Logica* (Servire's Encyclopaedie, Afd.: Logica, No. 37), 2nd rev. Ed. 92 pp. N.V. Servire, Den Haag, 1948.
[H]   *Wijsbegeerte der Wiskunde* (Philosophische Bibliotheek). 2nd entirely revised Ed. 388 pp. N.V. Standaard-Boekhandel, Antwerpen, N.V. Dekker & van de Vegt, Nijmegen, 1948.
[P]   Tarski, A. *Inleiding tot de logica en tot de methodeleer der deductieve wetenschappen* (revised edition in Dutch). XX + 260 pp. N.V. Noord-Hollandsche Uitg. Mij, Amsterdam, 1953; 2nd revised ed. 1964.
[S]   *La crise de la raison et la logique* (Collection de logique mathématique, Séries A, Fasc. XII). 52 pp. Gauthier-Villars, Paris; E. Nauwelaerts, Louvain, 1957.
[U]   *The Foundations of Mathematics*. A Study in the Philosophy of Science. XXVI + 722 pp. North-Holland Publ. Co., Amsterdam, 1959.
[V]   (with J. Piaget) *Epistémologie mathématique et psychologie*. Essai sur les relations entre la logique formelle et la pensée réelle. Presses Universitaires de France, Paris, 1961.
[W]   *Formal Methods*. An Introduction to Symbolic Logic and to the Study of Effective Operations in Arithmetic and Logic. XIV + 170 pp. D. Reidel Publishing Cy, Dordrecht, 1962.
[2]   'Klassieke en moderne Scheikunde – Van autonome wetenschap tot onderdeel der natuurkunde', *ANTW* 28 (1934/1935) 131–147 = *Annalen* 5 (1935) 35–51.
[69]   'Zomerconferentie 1953', *ANTW* 46 (1953/54) 41–45.
[69ª] 'Nominalisme in de hedendaagse logica', *Folia Civitatis* 14 febr. 1953.
[74]   'Kants Einteilung der Urteile in analytische und synthetische', *ANTW* 46, 253–264.
[76]   Dutch translation: A. Tarski, 'Het semantisch waarheidsbegrip en de grondslagen der semantiek', *Euclides* 30 (1954–1955).
[79]   'Semantic Entailment and Formal Derivability', *Mededelingen Kon. Ned. Akad. van Wet.*, Afd. lett., N.R. 18, no. 13 (1955).
[89]   'Monisme en pluralisme in logica en wiskunde', *ANTW* 48 (1955/56) 218–231 = *Annalen* 25 (1955) 34–47.
[94]   'Über Lockes "Allgemeines Dreieck"', *Kant-Studien* 48 (1956/57) 361–380.
[102] 'Le savoir déductif dans la pensée cartésienne', in *Descartes*, Cahiers de Royaumont, Phil. Nr. II, Paris 1957, pp. 141–153, 164–165.
[107] 'Geformaliseerde talen en normaal taalgebruik', *ANTW* 50 (1957/58) 265–276 = *Annalen* 29 (1958) 79–90.
[107ª] 'Naschrift', *ANTW* 50 (1957/58) 261–262.

[108] 'On Machines Which Prove Theorems', *Simon Stevin* **32** (1958) 49–60.
[120] 'Moderne logica', *Euclides* **34** (1958/59) 257–266.
[126] 'Completeness Results for Formal Systems', in *Proceedings of the Int. Congress of Mathematics* [Edinburgh, 14–21 August 1958], Cambridge 1960, pp. 281–288.

ABBREVIATIONS

ANTW = *Algemeen Nederlands Tijdschrift voor Wijsbegeerte en Psychologie* [of the articles taken up in this journal several appeared later, too, in the *Annalen van het Genootschap voor Critische* (afterwards: *Wetenschappelijke*) *Philosophie*].

PPR   = *Philosophy and Phenomenological Research.*

JSL   = *Journal of Symbolic Logic*

Annalen = *Annalen van het Genootschap voor Wetenschappelijke Philosophie.* Appearing in *ANTW*.

INDEX OF NAMES

INDEX OF SUBJECTS

SYNTHESE LIBRARY

Monographs on Epistemology, Logic, Methodology,
Philosophy of Science, Sociology of Science and of Knowledge, and on the
Mathematical Methods of Social and Behavioral Sciences

Editors:

DONALD DAVIDSON (Princeton University)
JAAKKO HINTIKKA (Academy of Finland and Stanford University)
GABRIËL NUCHELMANS (University of Leyden)
WESLEY C. SALMON (Indiana University)

‡PAUL WEINGARTNER and GERHARD ZECHA, *Induction, Physics, and Ethics. Proceedings and Discussions of the 1968 Salzburg Colloquium in the Philosophy of Science.* 1970, X + 382 pp. Dfl. 65.—

‡ROLF A. EBERLE, *Nominalistic Systems.* 1970, IX + 217 pp. Dfl. 42.—

‡JAAKKO HINTIKKA and PATRICK SUPPES, *Information and Inference.* X + 336 pp. Dfl. 60.—

‡KAREL LAMBERT, *Philosophical Problems in Logic. Some Recent Developments.* 1970, VII+176 pp. Dfl. 38.—

‡P. V. TAVANEC (ed.), *Problems of the Logic of Scientific Knowledge.* 1969, XII+ 429 pp. Dfl. 95.—

‡ROBERT S. COHEN and RAYMOND J. SEEGER (eds.), *Boston Studies in the Philosophy of Science.* Volume VI: *Ernst Mach: Physicist and Philosopher.* 1970, VIII+295 pp. Dfl. 38.—

‡MARSHALL SWAIN (ed.), *Induction, Acceptance, and Rational Belief.* 1970, VII+ 232 pp. Dfl. 40.—

‡NICHOLAS RESCHER et al. (eds.), *Essays in Honor of Carl G. Hempel. A Tribute on the Occasion of his Sixty-Fifth Birthday.* 1969, VII + 272 pp. Dfl. 46.—

‡PATRICK SUPPES, *Studies in the Methodology and Foundations of Science. Selected Papers from 1951 to 1969.* 1969, XII + 473 pp. Dfl. 70.—

‡JAAKKO HINTIKKA, *Models for Modalities. Selected Essays.* 1969, IX+220 pp. Dfl. 34.—

‡D. DAVIDSON and J. HINTIKKA: (eds.), *Words and Objections: Essays on the Work of W. V. Quine.* 1969, VIII + 366 pp. Dfl. 48.—

‡J. W. DAVIS, D. J. HOCKNEY, and W. K. WILSON (eds.), *Philosophical Logic.* 1969, VIII + 277 pp. Dfl. 45.—

‡ROBERT S. COHEN and MARX W. WARTOFSKY (eds.), *Boston Studies in the Philosophy of Science.* Volume V: *Proceedings of the Boston Colloquium for the Philosophy of Science 1966/1968.* 1969, VIII + 482 pp. Dfl. 58.—

p.t.o.

‡Robert S. Cohen and Marx W. Wartofsky (eds.), *Boston Studies in the Philosophy of Science*. Volume IV: *Proceedings of the Boston Colloquium for the Philosophy of Science 1966/1968*. 1969, VIII + 537 pp.   Dfl. 69.—

‡Nicholas Rescher, *Topics in Philosophical Logic*. 1968, XIV + 347 pp.   Dfl. 62.—

‡Günther Patzig, *Aristotle's Theory of the Syllogism. A Logical-Philological Study of Book A of the Prior Analytics*. 1968, XVII + 215 pp.   Dfl. 45.—

‡C. D. Broad, *Induction, Probability, and Causation. Selected Papers*. 1968, XI + 296 pp.
                                                                              Dfl. 48.—

‡Robert S. Cohen and Marx W. Wartofsky (eds.), *Boston Studies in the Philosophy of Science*. Volume III: *Proceedings of the Boston Colloquium for the Philosophy of Science 1964/1966*. 1967, XLIX + 489 pp.   Dfl. 65.—

‡Guido Küng, *Ontology and the Logistic Analysis of Language. An Enquiry into the Contemporary Views on Universals*. 1967, XI + 210 pp.   Dfl. 38.—

*Evert W. Beth and Jean Piaget, *Mathematical Epistemology and Psychology*. 1966.
XXII + 326 pp.   Dfl. 58.—

*Evert W. Beth, *Mathematical Thought. An Introduction to the Philosophy of Mathematics*. 1965, XII + 208 pp.   Dfl. 32.—

‡Paul Lorenzen, *Formal Logic*. 1965, VIII + 123 pp.   Dfl. 22.—

‡Georges Gurvitch, *The Spectrum of Social Time*. 1964, XXVI + 152 pp. Dfl. 20.—

‡A. A. Zinov'ev, *Philosophical Problems of Many-Valued Logic*. 1963, XIV + 155 pp.
                                                                              Dfl. 28.—

‡Marx W. Wartofsky (ed.), *Boston Studies in the Philosophy of Science*. Volume I: *Proceedings of the Boston Colloquium for the Philosophy of Science, 1961–1962*. 1963, VIII + 212 pp.   Dfl. 22.50

‡B. H. Kazemier and D. Vuysje (eds.), *Logic and Language. Studies dedicated to Professor Rudolf Carnap on the Occasion of his Seventieth Birthday*. 1962, VI + 246 pp.
                                                                              Dfl. 32.50

*Evert W. Beth, *Formal Methods. An Introduction to Symbolic Logic and to the Study of Effective Operations in Arithmetic and Logic*. 1962, XIV + 170 pp.   Dfl. 30.—

*Hans Freudenthal (ed.), *The Concept and the Role of the Model in Mathematics and Natural and Social Sciences. Proceedings of a Colloquium held at Utrecht, The Netherlands, January 1960*. 1961, VI + 194 pp.   Dfl. 30.—

‡P. L. R. Guiraud, *Problèmes et méthodes de la statistique linguistique*. 1960,
VI + 146 pp.   Dfl. 22.50

*J. M. Bocheński, *A Precis of Mathematical Logic*. 1959, X + 100 pp.   Dfl. 20.—

Sole Distributors in the U.S.A. and Canada:

*GORDON & BREACH, INC., 150 Fifth Avenue, New York, N.Y. 10011
‡HUMANITIES PRESS, INC., 303 Park Avenue South, New York, N.Y. 10010